-ON-TRENT ♥ BURNLEY ♥ CARLISLE ♥ GLASC
EICESTER ♥ WARWICK ♥ ━━━━━━━ RB
R ♥ CHESTER ♥ SHREW ┃┃┃┃┃┃┃┃┃┃ OL
NBURGH ♥ COVENTRY ┃ D0198637 ┃ DE
OGATE ♥ GRIMSBY ♥ SCUNTHORPE ━ ND
JRY ♥ DUNFERMLINE ♥ BOOTLE ♥ HAWICK ♥
♥ WHITBY ♥ ONCE BREWED ♥ STIRLING ♥
GAN ♥ ST HELENS ♥ BIRKENHEAD ♥ RIPON
♥ DOUGLAS ♥ STRANRAER ♥ WORKINGTON ♥
AND ♥ ROTHERHAM ♥ OLDHAM ♥ SALFORD
G ♥ TAMWORTH ♥ CANNOCK ♥ REDDITCH ♥
AMBE ♥ IMMINGHAM ♥ LEEK ♥ BLACKPOOL
MATLOCK ♥ PENRITH ♥ FORT WILLIAM ♥ W
MARTY ♥ SWAFFHAM ♥ STAVELEY ♥ MACCL
STER ♥ KENDAL ♥ ALNWICK ♥ GALCANTRY ♥
♥ DROITWICH ♥ SUTTON COLDFIELD ♥ UPTO
♥ POLESWORTH ♥ KIBWORTH BEAUCHAMP
SOAR ♥ WITHERNSEA ♥ SHEPSHED ♥ HEDO
RAMLINGTON ♥ BINGHAM ♥ MOULTON ♥ B
ER ♥ GREAT YARMOUTH ♥ BOSTON ♥ CROV
VHISTLE ♥ CUDWORTH ♥ ADWICK LE STREET
ARKET WEIGHTON ♥ HORNCASTLE ♥ STRENS
RTH-ON-TEES ♥ CATTERICK ♥ LOOTCHERBRA
LEATOR MOOR ♥ WEM ♥ GRANGE-OVER-SAN
♥ ANNAN ♥ GIRVAN ♥ AIRDRIE ♥ LINLITHC
TTERBURN ♥ GUNNERTON ♥ NEWBIGGIN-BY-
ETH ♥ PRUDHOE ♥ SACRISTON ♥ TRIMDON

It's NOT Grim up North

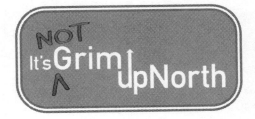

It's NOT Grim up North

JUDITH HOLDER

Foreword by

STUART MACONIE

BBC

BOOKS

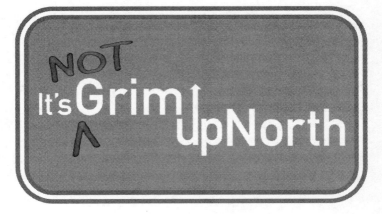

In memory of Miriam Hyman

This book is published to accompany the television series entitled *It's Grim Up North*, which was first broadcast in 2005. The series was produced by Liberty Bell Productions for BBC Television.

Executive producers: Judith Holder and Stuart Prebble
Produced and directed by Pip Banyard
Written by Judith Holder

Published by BBC Books, BBC Worldwide Limited, Woodlands, 80 Wood Lane, London W12 0TT

First published 2005

ISBN 0 563 52281 X

Commissioning editors: Shirley Patton and Stuart Cooper Project editor: Sarah Reece
Copy editor: Judith Scott Designer: Linda Blakemore
Picture researcher: Miriam Hyman Production controller: Peter Hunt

The publishers would like to thank those who gave permission to reproduce copyright material. Every effort has been made to contact copyright holders.

Set in Baskerville and Quay
Printed and bound in Great Britain by CPI Bath

For more information about this and other BBC books, please visit our website on www.bbcshop.com or telephone 08700 777 001.

Contents

For Northerners everywhere
(but North London is pushing it)

Foreword

I am delighted to have been asked by the fine, handsome, richly talented and mainly northern people behind this book to say a few words of introduction. I am honing them now, here on the veranda of my winter bolthole on the Cap d'Antibes, listening to the ice cracking gently in my Kir Royale and waiting for Monique – delightful girl – to bring me my *boudin noir à la Bury avec mushy peas Méditerranée*, my daily tribute, nay, homage to the cuisine of my native and beloved northwest. I hope to return there some day, perhaps when they have built a River Café in Chorley.

Only joking, cock! I am writing these words in the actual northwest of England. You can tell this because a thin drizzle, bolstered by gusting winds of up to 70 mph is rattling the windowpanes. To the Michael Winners, Brian Sewells and Simon Heffers of this world, such weather, as well as the lack of a decent cravat shop, is what makes the North a wilderness populated by oiks. Good. Let them believe what they will, as long it keeps them safely south of the Thames Valley, living off swan roulade and mead, or whatever it is they eat down there.

To misquote L P Hartley, inventor of jam and long-playing records and a great novelist to boot, 'the North is a foreign country: they do things differently there'. We talk to each other at bus stops and in shop queues, we wear boob tubes in December, and we drink Mild, a kind of less pretentious Guinness.

And there are certain traits and customs of the South that we simply do not get, which are as alien to us as the fashions of the Hindu Kush or the songs of the Kalahari nomads. We do not get Chas and Dave, even ironically, because, lest we forget, they were absolutely rubbish. We have no particular affection for class-traitor gangsters like the Kray Twins, Mad Frankie Fraser or indeed for the irritating public schoolboys like Guy Ritchie who lionize them. We don't 'do' Rugby Union, having a vastly superior, faster, more entertaining alternative, played by skilled athletes rather than hulking poshos called Rob and Will and Sebastian and Montague, who are letting off a bit of steam before they're 'called to the Bar' or they 'take over Dad's practice', or some such nonsense.

No one in the North has that ridiculous Jonathan Woss/Woy Jenkins speech affectation. Note I say 'affectation', not 'impediment'. In the North any such bizarre linguistic tic would be beaten out of you with gusto by jeering classmates at the bus stop every day until you learned to speak properly. And by speak properly I mean to flatten every vowel until you could slip it under a door, and to trim off the unnecessary and indulgent bit of the word 'the' to make for more brisk and efficient phrases, such as 'Where's t'hammer?', 'Look on t'Internet' and 'I see t'Alle orchestra is premiering a new work by t'acclaimed Estonian minimalist Arvo Pärt. Should be a reet good, if challenging, neet out.'

My dander's up now and I've obviously had a few so let me just say in conclusion – southerners, who needs 'em? Soft, pigeon-eating, 'lazy r'-pronouncing scum, all of them. And, another thing, the South starts at Stafford, right? Any one from below Crewe is a tosser. No, make that below Warrington. In fact, I can have anyone in this book now. Come on, pal. Outside – now! And your mates!

Ah, here comes Monique with my Armagnac *digestif* and a copy of the Lancashire *Evening Post*'s excellent *Football Pink*. And so, hoping you enjoy this wise and witty book, I bid you a fond 'ah'll sithee'.

Stuart Maconie

Introduction

Dear friend in the North,

You will have picked up this book because either:

You live up North and are fed up with people down South having a laugh at your expense and pretending that the North is still in the Dark Ages and that you have only just got street lighting, sleep eight to a bed and are still waiting for colour telly.

OR

You come from the North and are forced to live in the South and are keen to read something about your beloved motherland.

Dear friend in the South,

You, on the other hand, will have picked up this book for different reasons, either:

You live down South but are thinking of buying this book for someone who lives up North (and has a sense of humour).

OR

You live in the South and enjoy a little snigger about the people who live in the North – if this is the case, you'll be disappointed.

OR MAYBE

You are in a bookshop sheltering from the rain in the Lake District or North Wales or the Scottish Highlands, curious as to what the hell this cheekily titled book is all about and wishing you had packed a mac.

Whatever the reason, I commend this book to you all (well, I would, wouldn't I?) on the basis that the North–South divide is no longer a matter of drawing a straight line across the country through the middle of Watford and being done with it. This division within our country is getting more and more complicated, but it persists because of a combination of misunderstanding, anger and sheer bigotry. I blame the media (doesn't everyone?). Or society. Or both. Either way, it needs a bit of straightening out, or at the very least it needs to be given an airing so that we can all have a good laugh at one another's expense … which is the next best thing.

As you might have guessed, this book is neither a scientific study nor a result of meticulous cross-referencing of acres of statistics. It represents a point of view … *my* point of view. I live in the North and I love it. I don't mind admitting that I have been a little economical with the truth here and there, and I have to confess that sometimes I have been a touch inventive with some of the data. Apart from anything else, once someone shows me a table or a vector or a series of figures, I get a little bit special needs and a little bit number blind, so I generally pick out the things that either interest me or support my argument – should have gone into politics probably. My main justification, though, is that I reckon it's our turn up in the North to spin things our way for a change, and so I have seized this opportunity to talk about our beloved part of the country unimpeded.

Whichever camp you belong to, there is little doubt that the trouble with Britain today is that the people who live in London and the southeast – anywhere within the M25, to be precise – think they run the country. Trouble is, they *do* run the country, but the rest of us have had enough.

Don't they know that only a small fraction of the population – less than a quarter, in fact – live in the bottom right-hand corner of the country? The North has twice the population of London. There are more people living in Yorkshire and Greater Manchester than London but the way this country operates you'd think it was the other way round. Because all the major investment, businesses and decision-making are concentrated in the South and that's also where all the decent airports, art galleries, museums and major sporting venues are. And if that wasn't enough, Londoners will even have the blooming Olympics, too, right there on their not-very-well-scrubbed doorstep. Which means that we'll all end up paying for improvements to the infrastructure that will be left behind for *them* to enjoy. OK, so Royal Ascot moved to York for a nice sensible outing in 2005, but even when Wembley gets rebuilt someone decides to rebuild it in Wembley.

Now let me tell you southerners about that other place in the UK. Those of us who live here call it 'the North'. Those of you who live in the South insultingly call it 'the grim north' or 'the frozen north'. It includes Scotland and Northern Ireland, of course, as well as the northeast and the northwest of England, and probably (in a cultural or psychological sense) Wales, the Midlands, East Anglia and the West Country as well. In your mind, it probably all looks the same, maybe something like the picture at the top of the next page.

Chimneys, slag heaps, dole-queues, whippets, disused factories, prams in rivers, sink estates … and all looking as if they've been shaken up in one of those snowy blizzard ornaments. That's what you think it looks like in the North. And who can blame you? Because that's all you ever see on the telly.

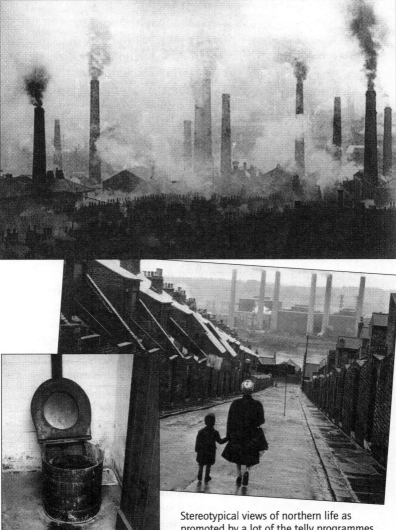

Stereotypical views of northern life as promoted by a lot of the telly programmes you see down south.

And in your mind you think we live in cobbled streets, in back-to-back houses where the plumbing tends to be located somewhere outside, whereas we are more likely to live in pleasant, open countryside in something that looks like this.

You're so last week. In terms of bringing southerners up to speed, there is some work still left to do. Which is what I intend to do in this book. Which is not to say that we want you to read it and rush up here and invade us. Quite the opposite. Or *au contraire*, as they say in Cheshire. We don't want to encourage you to come up north, so best not to disillusion you on that score. There isn't anything worth visiting up here. Nothing whatsoever. Honest. So please don't visit any of our ancient monuments, any of our beaches, any of our historic towns and cities. Please don't bother to take any interest whatsoever in our architecture or our museums, art galleries or concert halls. We're certain you wouldn't want to buy anything in our shops. Eat any of our rather funny food. Try any of our beer. Go to any of our sports events or festivals. Travel on any of our public transport. No, no, perish the thought. Certainly we from 'the North' don't want to say anything in this book that would lure you up here – with your manic driving habits and your congestion charge and your bad manners and funny way of talking, you are more than welcome … to stay away.

No, we just want whatever idiots are taking decisions in the mother of parliaments to notice that not everyone – and that's about 75% of us – lives where you live. That not everyone even *wants* to live where you live. And not everyone in this country feels that Britain revolves around that stupid, oversized grid-locked roundabout called the M25.

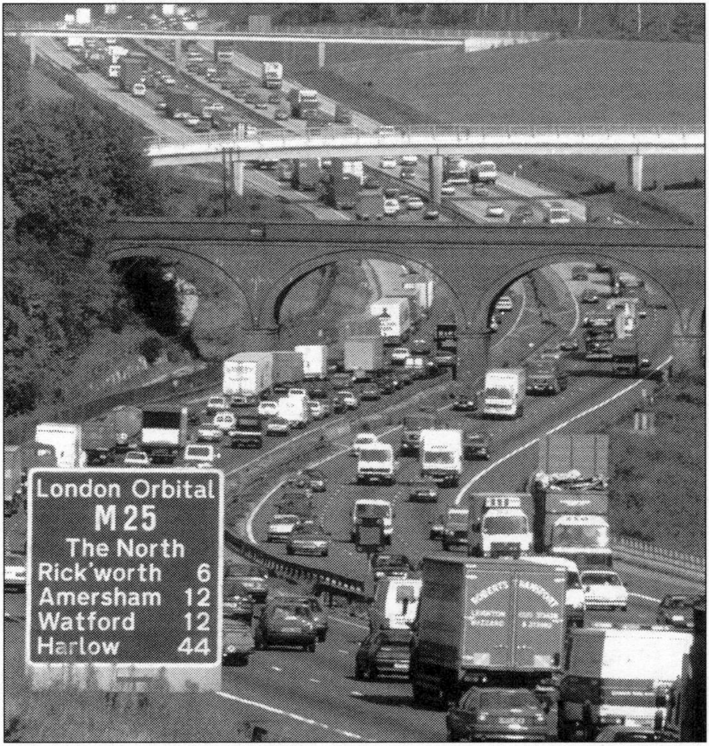

Another lovely ride out of London.

That's what we call a lovely ride out up North.

So that's what this book is all about.

It's about why we don't want to have to go via Heathrow when we want to go from Tyneside to New York. And it's about why, when we have important events and openings, we don't want to spend our whole time seeing television coverage of those near London just because it's where you live and not where we live.

Let's put some of the more bigoted of these southern prejudices to bed once and for all ... for instance:

- There is officially more fresh air up north because we have over half of the entire country's national parks.

- The North has more heritage sites than the whole of Kenya.

- Yorkshire has more ancient history than Egypt (actually I made that one up but it sounded good and anyway Yorkshire has better tea bags).

This book is about persuading you, our friends in the South, to stop lording it over us and referring to the North as if it's stuck in the Ice Age – believe me, we are not still covered in woad and roaming the land with picks and axes. And another thing: you need to stop thinking that property is so cheap up here that you can hoover up an entire street with the proceeds of the sale of a single semi in Surbiton, or that there's such a glut that you can buy one and get one free.

You are going to have to get used to the fact that most of the North–South differences have gone and they are selling as much designer gear in Knutsford as they do in Knightsbridge these days, albeit in larger sizes. Tatton in Cheshire has the highest income per capita in the UK, and in Alderley Edge they buy more champagne than anywhere else in the country. I could point you in the direction of a middle-class enclave in every northern town and city, complete with smart restaurants, bookshops and million-pound houses. OK, well not Cleethorpes, perhaps, but you are just as likely to find people enjoying their frappuccinos and *pains au chocolat* in the pavement cafés of Leeds and Liverpool as you would in Hampstead or Highgate. All this means more tourists and the new Lonely Planet Guide compares our northern cities to Barcelona, Rome and Florence – 'urban tourism is not about beaches, it's about bars, music and being in a cosmopolitan atmosphere'.

To sum up: what qualifies me to write this book? Well, as a Brummie, I am perfectly placed – with a foot in both camps – to examine the North–South divide from personal experience. We Brummies are the filling in the North–South sandwich and we don't half take some flak. Northerners think we are all southern wusses and southerners don't know where Birmingham is and, what's more, they don't care. To them we're all one big molten lump of 'north'.

My main reason for writing this book is that I now live in Northumberland, which is one of the most beautiful counties in Britain, and I'm fed up with having to justify my decision to settle here to all those poor deluded people who can't bear the thought of anyone being so far away from the sacred south. Well, what I say to them is that what I like in life is plenty of space and fresh air, a stunning coastline, and the vibrant city of Newcastle-upon-Tyne just down the road. And I'm not moving.

CHAPTER ONE

The North–South Divide

They may be awash with swanky river fronts, with their trendy galleries and smart new coffee shops, in Gateshead and Glasgow, but make no mistake: the North–South divide is still alive and well. The way we speak, the way we dress, the food we eat – there are enough differences between a typical northerner and a typical southerner to fill a book. Well, this book really.

A Question of Geography

Before we can embark on a discussion of the distinction between the North and the South of Great Britain, we need to define our terms. Because it's vastly more complicated than it used to be when Minnie Caldwell and Ena Sharples sat in the snug at the Rovers, pale ales and hairnets aplenty, and when London was swinging its miniskirts at the world and the rest of the country looked on in envy and amazement. The North has officially changed, and the South is no longer a place we look at with awesome wonder and envy. And so it all needs some re-examination. When I think of the South now, I think of a series of ring roads and solid conurbation that is so built up that you never see a blade of grass, where the people are suspicious of their neighbours and where they all eat funny foreign food. The North is the place where there is lots of wild, open countryside and some serious fresh air, where the people are nice and friendly (even towards the odd tourist – which is saying something), and where women wander the streets in a dress the size of a tea towel in sub-zero temperatures and still party. There, that's nice and scientific, isn't it?

But if you insist on geography, then roughly speaking in my book (well literally in fact) the South is the bottom right-hand corner of the UK, with London somewhere in the middle. It definitely includes the so-called Home Counties (Surrey, Kent and Essex and what used to be Middlesex) and spreads out in all directions to include some places where you might expect to find green wellies, waxed Barbour jackets and black labradors. Places like the New Forest or the Cotswolds, for example. For the sake of convenience, why don't we just say that anywhere within an easy day trip of London is the South and everywhere else is the North?

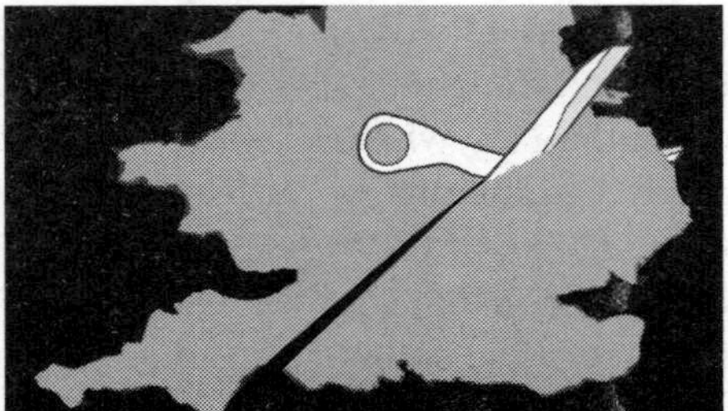

This leaves us with Devon, Cornwall and Wales, which I think of as a sort of honorary north because Whitehall obviously doesn't give a toss about the people living there. Surely they all run hotels, tea shops or cashmere sweater outlets? They must be rich, then. Like the farmers. Being so far away from London, these places don't even merit a decent motorway. This means that those of us who do venture that far south or west have to spend four hours on a dual carriageway nose to tail to get a glimpse of the sea, but then Whitehall thinks it's only for two weeks of the year, and the people who make the decisions in the capital all go to Tuscany in August rather than St Ives or Tenby so they have no idea how bad the roads are there in high summer. Out of sight, out of mind as usual.

So that's it: Devon, Cornwall and Wales are part of the honorary north, though obviously not for the people who have second homes there who simply drive down from Fulham on a Friday night and expect the locals to have put the wheelie bin back in for them without actually offering anything to the community in return.

So within our scheme of things, the Isles of Scilly and the Channel Islands, which are further south than anywhere else in Great Britain, are in fact so far off the radar that they are not just in the North, they are the far honorary north. Keep up! Along with most of Scotland, the Outer Hebrides and the Shetland Islands, which actually *are* further north than anywhere else in Great Britain, they are the far north. Get the picture? Oh well, suit yourselves.

Part of the problem of the North–South divide, geographically speaking, is that southerners know so very little about the rest of the country. Anything north of Lancaster Gate is a struggle for them, never mind Lancaster itself. For the *It's Grim Up North* TV series we did our own 'stick the tail on the donkey' type experiment (no expense spared). We asked a batch of southerners to stick the names of some well-known northern towns on a map of Great Britain and I have to say the results were (predictably) shocking. One bright spark placed Stockton-on-Tees in the Highlands of Scotland, another put Nuneaton as a suburb of Manchester, and one thought Doncaster and Darlington were the same place. Let's hope they don't drive National Express coaches for a living.

I once saw a Sky news report and I think it was when Rochdale had drawn some big southern club, it might have been Chelsea, in the FA Cup, three or four years ago. And they'd sent this smirking nitwit to Rochdale, and the tone of his report, well, it was like they'd sent a man to Borneo. Now, I know exactly where Rochdale is, actually. So do most of the north of England, you know. And I thought, 'Can you imagine on a news report someone saying, "Now, most people probably wonder where Guildford is."' Well, I don't know where Guildford is. Why should I have any idea where Guildford is? It means nothing to me. But there's an assumption that we ought to. At the end of the piece this reporter said, 'Well, they'll be hoping tomorrow to put Rochdale on the map.' As if this city of hundreds of thousands of people wasn't there! ***Stuart Maconie***

I'm not saying that people in the North know any more about the South – I imagine if we did the same test in Yorkshire then few people could put Salisbury or Oxford or Colchester on the right bit of the map – but then we don't swan about pretending we're all superior. (Mind you, whose idea was it to put Leeds Castle in Kent?)

The Watford Gap

So where does the North, for most people, actually start? When you ask, people often say Watford, or the Watford Gap, or the A1. It's become a bit of a cliché, though if they're really, really snobby then they'll come up with something like Islington. You know who I mean – Jeremy and Tristram and Phoebe, the double-barrelled lot, the ones with the floppy hair and a bijou pied-à-terre in Chelsea plus a place in the country. They think the North is so – well, vulgar probably. In fact, anyone's idea of where the border is varies wildly, and it depends, as you might expect, on whether they class themselves as northerners or not.

I think some people used to say north of Watford because for people living in London that was about as far north as they could reasonably visualize civilization extended to. It was a bit like the Flat Earth Society, really, and beyond that was no-man's-land, so the Watford Gap became the frontier for the wild north.
William Roache

You used to class anything north of Birmingham as the North, and gradually over the years it became north of Watford – a line from Watford probably down to Bristol was the North. Now it's anything outside the southeast is the North and very shortly it will be anything outside the M25 will be the North.
Noddy Holder

I know exactly where the North starts, it starts north of Hyde Park; it starts at Oxford Street. Anything north of Oxford Street is ridiculous. ***Michael Winner***

So it seems that for most people (rather than those who come up with eccentric suggestions like north of Oxford Street) the North really does start at Watford. Now Watford in Hertfordshire is just a dreary southern town whose claim to fame is their moderately successful football club, which was, until recently, owned by our very own singer–songwriter with a range of idiosyncratic hairstyles, Elton John. This Watford is in the commuter-belt county of Hertfordshire. But, confusingly, this is not the same Watford as in the Watford Gap. There is a Watford Gap in Staffordshire, near Lichfield, but we don't need to go there as it's definitely in the North. The Watford with the Gap that we are looking for turns out to be a nice village in rural Northamptonshire, about a mile off the M1, not far from Daventry. And there's not a lot of people know that.

❝ *I've got no idea what the Watford Gap is unless it's some kind of cultural gap in Watford. Perhaps in the olden days in Watford they just realized there was no cultural excellence, so it's a kind of civilization gap.* ***Mark Radcliffe***

❝ *What is the Watford Gap? Watford Gap's a service station, isn't it? But I don't know what the Gap is. And it's nowhere near Watford. Isn't it somewhere like Peterborough? I don't know what the Watford Gap really is. When I think of the Watford Gap, though, I think more Julie's Pantry than I think massive social schism.* ***Stuart Maconie***

So that's it. Watford Gap is a service station on the M1, between junctions 16 and 17. In fact it was the nation's first service station – impressed, or what? It had a reputation for being a bit grotty back in the old days, though I am told things have improved tremendously since Roadchef took it over in 1995. (I'm not stupid – they sell a lot of nice cheese-and-tomato sarnies and anyway, they might send the heavies round.) They've got a bit of an uphill struggle if they want to change their image because the place has now entered public consciousness by way of an unfortunate bit of Cockney rhyming slang. Yes, you've guessed it. Watford Gap = 'crap'. Interesting that cockneys decided that the start of the North is to be linked with crapness or crapicity or whatever the noun is.

In the cause of historical research I have decided to put you all right about the Watford Gap because this sad, neglected place deserves better. So here goes. It all began with the Romans. Some 2000 years ago they built an earthwork right across the country from Bristol to Skegness – which means a hilly mound like the one you dig when you are planting potatoes but much much bigger – in order to secure the territory that they had conquered to the south. Somewhere along this line of defence was a place called the Watford Gap. (There was a bit of a craze for these hilly mounds evidently since Offa built a similar division between England and Wales in 784 and called it Offa's Dyke – it took him 12 years to build, sort of the equivalent of building a new motorway, but this one divided the East from the

West.) Eventually, as we all know, the Romans marched northwards until they hit Scotland. Which accounts for Hadrian's Wall. They built that between 122 and 126 to stop the barbarous tribes (not the Scots – they came later) from hammering them. But the Watford Gap lived on in folklore, even after the Romans abandoned their earthy division, and so it's more or less been taken as the natural North–South divide ever since. Being an earthwork, though, it proved much less durable than Hadrian's Wall. It probably collapsed under the pressure of all those southerners trying to barge their way into the North to find some decent chips.

The last surviving section of the original Roman earthwork was used as a landfill site during the construction of the service stations for Britain's first motorway, the M1, in 1959. All that remains is a small plaque on the overpass of the service area that bears its name – not a very glamorous end, is it? Although we hear there are plans to turn the cold snacks and sandwich section into a World Heritage Site.

Some people argue that it would be a good idea to settle this North–South matter once and for all and saw the country in half somewhere around the Watford Gap, allowing the North and the South to drift apart officially. Then Watford Gap would be Watford-Gap-on-Sea, which would be nice for the people who live there. They'd have a new ferry crossing and everything, which would make it distinctly harder for southerners to venture northwards. Plus, it would keep some of the French out. Nice plan.

Sawing the country in half could turn out to be a bit costly, but what about drawing a dividing line somewhere else? We could build a new version of Hadrian's Wall and this one would keep the southerners at bay. We already have a natural outline for this new barrier and it's called the M25. That's it – we could confine all southerners to the area within the M25. They would only be allowed to use the exits if they had a visa and went through a simple checkpoint process. Then they'd have to pay a toll like they do on the M6 toll road now. That would definitely be a step in the right direction.

> *I think perhaps you should have to show your birth certificate at the toll booths and if you are born anywhere south of Coventry ... well, perhaps turning people back would be a bit extreme, but certainly I think you should be charged more. I don't think people could refute the logic in that.* **Mark Radcliffe**

The Magnetic Pull of the North

Traditionally, the North is a place where people know a thing or two about pies and pork scratchings and where the women are genetically modified to withstand the cold when they go out wearing next to nothing in the middle of winter. Let's call it the motherland. This place acts as a sort of magnet that attracts natives and newcomers alike and exerts a powerful influence over the country as a whole, mostly through the medium of *Coronation Street* and Man U. As they used to say in a proverb in the mid-nineteenth century: 'What Manchester says today, the rest of England says tomorrow.'

Wherever you draw the North–South dividing line, one thing's for sure: as soon as they get to their own mythical personal border, people from the North always experience the thrill of anticipation mixed with nostalgia that hits every expat when they return to the motherland.

> *If I'm driving back up home I feel like I'm back up north when I cross the Manchester Ship Canal. I have this thing where*

when I get to Fort Dunlop on the M6, I salute. I mean, it's partly a stupid thing like touching wood. I have to salute because it means goodbye to the South, you're in the Midlands and I'm saying hello to the Midlands. And I've probably done it for 20 years now and the kids look at me sometimes and I say, 'That's what you do, that's what you have to do, you're saying you're back, you're back home.' ***Wayne Hemingway***

When I go back to Derbyshire and I cross the Trent, either by road bridge or by rail bridge, I see the river below me and I think I'm home, we're in the North. The North is north of the Trent. ***Roy Hattersley***

Once you see the proper place names start to come by the side of the train, or once you hear the vowels start to get a bit flatter, or once the countryside starts to get more interesting, I do start to think I am in God's own country again. Which is probably pathetic, but you know, we're very sentimental, us northerners. ***Stuart Maconie***

It's a funny thing, but I have heard that southerners sometimes get nostalgic in this way too, though goodness knows why. Hilaire Belloc (born in France, educated in

Birmingham and at Oxford, Liberal MP for Salford) certainly did. In 1920 he wrote a poem about it called 'The South Country'.

> When I am living in the Midlands
>   That are sodden and unkind,
> I light my lamp in the evening:
>   My work is left behind;
> And the great hills of the South Country
>   Come back into my mind.

The Middle of the Road

The poor benighted Midlands. Where does all this talk of the North–South divide leave them? Where do we place Birmingham and the Black Country? Are they in the North or are they in the South? Well, that's a tricky one, and for people who live in Dudley or Sutton Coldfield or even Northampton, it's a bit of a sore point.

“ *In spite of its name, Northampton's south, I think. There's just something southern about it, whereas Birmingham's north. It's like the planets and gravity, you know, the gravitational force. So I think Birmingham's gravitational force isn't London but if you get a bit further south it is. Take Northampton Development Corporation's slogan – 'Only 60 miles by road or rail' – now it didn't say where from or where to but it obviously means London.*
Stuart Maconie

“ *I think the Midlands is much more akin to the North than it is to the South, mainly through its working-class roots. The Midlands was the start of the industrial revolution and so we always considered ourselves as the gritty north.* ***Noddy Holder***

If you think the North gets a bad press, you should try living in Birmingham, the city of a thousand trades as it's known. Everyone has a go at the Brummies. Even when they finally got around to doing what they should have done years ago and pulled down the Bull Ring, people are still rude about the place – always have been and always will be, I suppose. As Mrs Elton says in Jane Austen's *Emma*: 'One has not great hopes from Birmingham, I always say there is something direful in the sound.' So nothing new there, then.

❝ *Birmingham does get it from all sides because northerners regard it as the South and southerners regard it as the North. It's 'cos it's bang in the middle of the country. And that speaks of a certain kind of dullness, if you see what I mean. No one ever gets excited about the middle of anything, do they?* ***Stuart Maconie***

❝ *I think the thing with Birmingham is that it is sort of the middle child of the country. You've got the northerners who are quite hearty and go-getting, like a first child, and then you've got the spoilt whiny southerners, who are like the baby sibling who came much later. And then you've got the stoic middle child, which is Birmingham, and whatever Birmingham does, however hard she/he tries, nobody's that impressed. I know what that's like, I'm a middle child, too. Birmingham, I understand.* ***Jenny Eclair***

Birmingham has always had a hard time – blitzed to bits in the Second World War and then taken for a ride by the planners from hell in the Sixties, who decided in their wisdom to demolish the marvellous glass-roofed Victorian New Street Station, so much stunning architecture and the Central Library.

❝ *It's like the proverbial explosion in a bad-taste factory. You can't understand why somebody went in there in the late 1960s and early 1970s and just said to themselves, 'I am going to punish a million or so people who live round here by putting up some of the ugliest buildings I can conceive of.' I think the nicest thing to do with Birmingham is to evacuate the people, raze it to the ground and start again.* ***Simon Heffer***

Because Birmingham's wealth in the middle of the twentieth century was based on car production, these Philistines, these so-called planners for the future, were so enamoured of anything on four wheels that they built a series of interlocking ring roads, underpasses and flyovers in and around the city by way of homage to the internal combustion engine. This worship of the motorcar left the poor pedestrians to find their own way around as best they could. If you were on foot it was not unusual to be faced with a three-mile detour through a maze of graffiti-covered, litter-strewn subways – and that was just to get to the pub on the other side of the dual carriageway. So fast-moving and racetrack-like were the roads in the centre of Birmingham that the city even indulged in its own Formula One event, which was officially identical to the one in Monte Carlo but with more vimto … but oh, I forgot, it's miles from the sea and it's a place where the sun never shines.

❝ *I think I have only stayed one night in Birmingham, which was memorably horrific. The whole place was memorably horrific, it was sort of motorways and hideous buildings – unrelieved eyesore, unrelieved visual toilet. Now I don't know about the people, bless them, they are probably quite sweet, really, but I remember going into a coffee bar in a hotel, because we were doing interviews, and this coffee bar was done out like it was a seaside port. There were nets and there were barrels and there was a little picture of the sea and I thought, 'What are they doing? They are in the middle of Birmingham in some basement dump and they are trying to kid us we are by the sea?' I mean, what is it with these people in Birmingham?* **Michael Winner**

It's such a popular stereotype – that Birmingham is just one massive car-choked sprawl with the ugliest architecture (and accents) in the country – but people don't realize that it has more open green space than London and more canals even than Venice. So yes, Birmingham has lots of lovely canals with proper snazzy walks alongside them and views and gondolas and everything. You can now hire your own personal gondolier – only £100 an hour for two, with champagne thrown in. Some of the venues sound a little off-putting though – like the Gas Street Basin, which is not exactly St Mark's Square, but hey, it's a big improvement.

Another place to avoid on the way to Britain's second city is Spaghetti Junction. It is a road planner's wet dream and a motorist's vision of hell. One false move and you end up in Ipswich.

“ *If ever I have to go into Birmingham I groan inwardly. How am I going to find my way around? And getting off Spaghetti Junction or whatever it's called is a nightmare, and I've been round and round the Bull Ring trying to find my way out. I think that is why Birmingham possibly has a bad image.* **William Roache**

So Birmingham's tragedy is that it's neither one thing nor the other. When Brummies go north they are treated like southern wusses and if they go south they are lumped in with all the other illiterate northerners. How fair is that? Birmingham was responsible for *Crossroads,* for goodness'

Don't knock Birmingham – it's not quite Venice, but it's well worth a visit ...

... although you may have trouble getting there via the notorious Spaghetti Junction.

sake. And it has more than its fair share of successful comedians and comic actors – Lenny Henry, Julie Walters, Meera Syal, Jasper Carrott, Frank Skinner …

I'm a Brummie myself, which I suppose puts me in the ideal position to write about the North–South divide. But nothing's ever simple, is it? The fact is, Birmingham itself has its very own geographical and cultural divide. If you come from Solihull like me, then you'll know all about it. The answer lies in the postcode. And though I say so myself, Brummies or Silhillians can be the most hellishly snobbish people in the world; we could certainly give those snooty southerners a run for their money. So be warned: the next time you go to Solihull, don't make the mistake of thinking you're in Birmingham. Or if you do think it, just keep your mouth shut.

How to Know Where You Are

Maybe this would be a good place to try and identify some definitive features of the North and the South. For example, you know you are in the North when …

- You have more than one hot water bottle in the kitchen drawer
- You ask for brown toast and people find you the slice of white toast that looks the darkest
- People know what to do with their lard
- People talk to you straight and don't use stupid phrases like 'forgive me … ' when they're about to insult you or 'heads up' when they are about to say something important
- You can park your car outside your house
- You can find breathtaking scenery without having to get in the car for two hours
- People ask if you do a reduction for cash
- You go home for your tea before you go out on the town
- You start to notice that the hills are a decent height
- You are comfortable in just a T-shirt in the snow.

" *England has got about 200 hills of any decent size, and in fact four over 3000 feet, and all of them are in the north-west. Anywhere south of Manchester and it's so flat that on a clear day you can see across to France. It's just fields and motorways all the way to the Channel. And don't say the Chilterns and all that, that's just a camber in the road.* ***Stuart Maconie***

When I was younger I was unlucky enough to experience London and the southeast at first hand. I didn't know what the Home Counties were, thought they were a make of

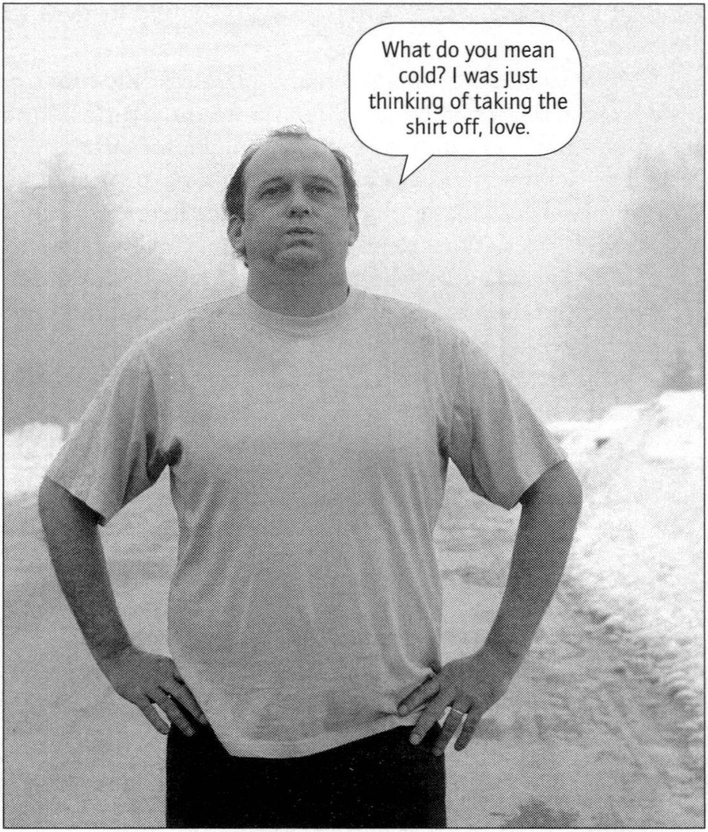

butter, but any fool can see it's not proper countryside down there. I mean, you wouldn't have caught Alfred Wainwright tramping up some namsy-pamsy hill in Berkshire, would you? And when you do go for a hike in the South there are so many other ramblers out for the day that you all have to walk single file. Not like the North. Some areas up here are so empty that you could get lost for days. They'd have to send a St Bernard with a bottle of brandy round its neck to find you.

People looking for the green and pleasant land that used to be Great Britain can still find it in the North. They will find it in the mountains of Scotland, the fells of the Lake District, the dales of Derbyshire and on the moors of Northumberland. These places are not just magical landscapes with marvellous clean air. There are lovely people here, too, nice, friendly, chatty folk – and you'll find some jolly good pub lunches and, in places, some stunning top-of-the-range food and restaurants. And yet to hear some of them southerners talk you'd think that the North still looked like it did a hundred years ago.

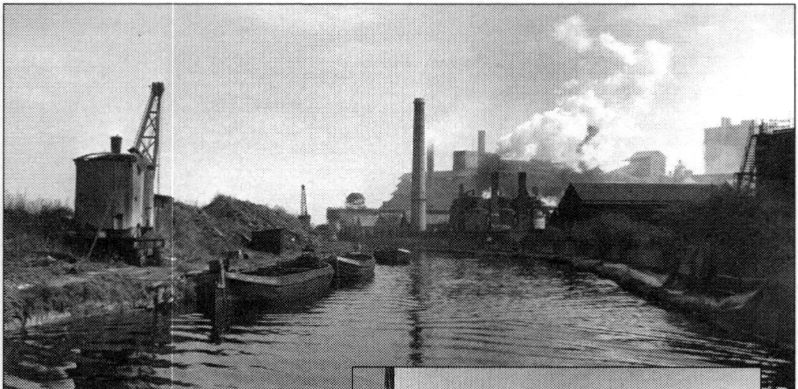

To hear some southerners talk you'd think the North still looked like this (above) ...

... instead of like trendy Newcastle, which was voted one of the top ten partying places in the world (right).

On the other hand you know you are in the South when …

- You see people paying for their groceries, even in the 10 items lane, with a credit card, and they take about 20 minutes doing it
- You blow your nose and find black snot on your hanky

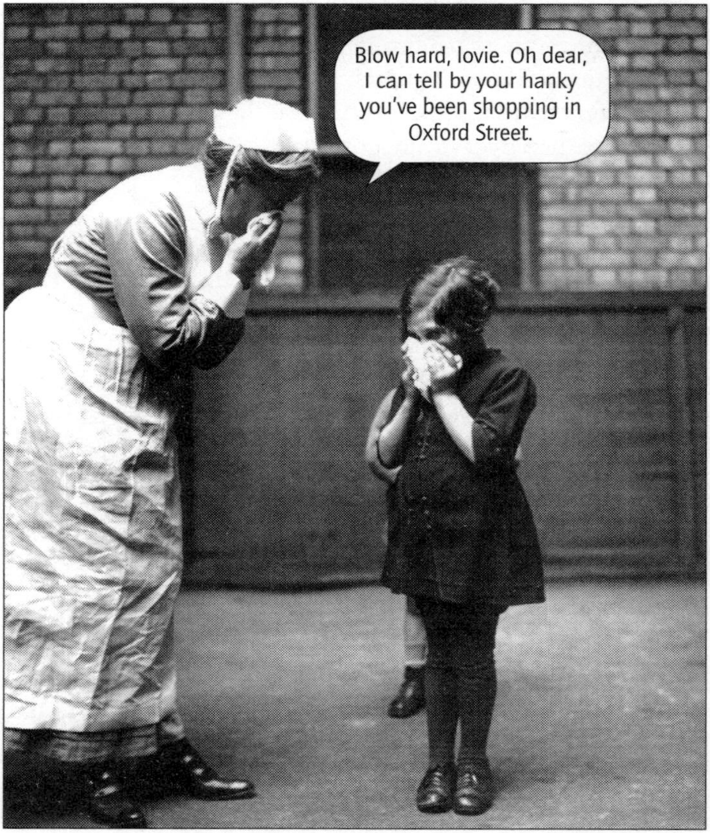

- You discover there are more life coaches or feng shui experts in the phone book than plumbers
- You see snooty signs on people's gates saying, 'No casual callers' or 'No turning'
- The doctor packs you off to a counsellor at a moment's notice – I mean, what's wrong with a nice long walk with a friend?
- Bus shelters are built in a mock-Tudor style
- People's wheelie bins have a leafy camouflage cover
- You realize the place is full of hideous children in silly uniforms and straw boaters, and parents who send their children *away* to school
- You find that everything costs about three times as much as it should do.

Of course, geography is one thing, but money is another, because one thing you can be sure of is that people in the South, and in particular in London, earn a great deal more than we do up North. The cultural differences between the North, the honorary north and the South are getting narrower, since all our high streets have more or less identical shops on them, we watch the same soaps, read the same books and buy the same pointless hair products, but in other ways the differences are as large and as gaping as ever. And these differences are largely economic.

As you would expect, London is the most expensive place to live in the UK, but then average earnings there are considerably more than the national average – no, *astonishingly* higher than the average. For as long as Payfinder have been gathering salary comparisons, London has seen significantly higher wages than the rest of the country. According to the Office of National Statistics the average wage for the country as a whole in 2004 was £22,440.

The typical Londoner earns a staggering £8500 per year more than this. Wales is the cheapest place to live, at 6.9% below the national average. But as people there earn 10% below the national average, most of them are worse off than workers anywhere else.

The following information is the nearest you can get to a guide to which regions are the best off, which regions have the most disposable income, and which the least. A sort of wealth index for the country:

Region	*Average salary*	*Wealth index*
London	£30,984	128.6
South East	£25,221	107.2
Scotland	£22,230	104.7
East Midlands	£22,528	103.1
West Midlands	£22,529	102.7
North West	£22,102	101.7
Yorks & Humber	£21,085	99.9
East of England	£21,936	99.0
Wales	£20,391	97.9
South West	£22,205	97.8
North East	£20,353	96.6
Northern Ireland	£17,366	82.3
Average	**£22,411**	**100**

In London rents are higher, weekly groceries are more expensive, the cost of living is higher, but still taking all this into account most people in London and the South are better off than most people in the North. They have more choices: more job choices, more life choices and more disposable income. Which is not to say that there aren't people in the South who aren't desperately in need of more money – quite the opposite. Of course, the differences between the very rich and the very poor in the South is predictably much larger than in the North. London has the highest number of rich people in the country (39%) and also the highest number of poor (32%), which only leaves about two families in the middle somewhere. There are nearly twice as many people living in low-income households in London and the southeast than in the North. Which makes the South all the more wretched a place to be poor.

Movers and Shakers

I suppose it should come as no surprise that England is still run from London. Of all the money Whitehall or London controls, a small fraction is given over to regional government offices to organize – £9 billion in 2003 in fact, out of a total government expenditure of £421 billion. Until someone organizes a sensible series of regional assemblies, it's likely to stay that way. But once in a while the politicians, the ones who make all the big decisions about the North but don't actually live here, really do look stupid. They just can't help themselves. And that always cheers us northerners up.

Let me tell you a story. A prospective candidate (let's call him Politician X) looks for a safe seat, somewhere way, way up in the North or the northeast, like Hartlepool – and then, shock, horror, he has to go there. Politician X flies, of course. His time is precious, so he's not going to want to hang around on a draughty platform wondering whether the train's going to leave on time and, if it does, whether it's going to take all day to get there.

Politician X has to look as if he knows about the natives he is planning to represent, the local issues and all that, so he mugs up on notes prepared for him by smart Oxbridge types on the 50-minute flight up. Then it's off in the chauffeur-driven car to spend a couple of days schmoozing the local party hacks and sitting in smoky village halls trying to look as though he understands even half of what his future constituents are saying to him and bingo! – some chummy at Number 10 calls in a few favours and gets him the nomination anyway, so it's all been worth the effort.

During the election campaign, up he flies again for a whirlwind weekend of wooing the voters and this time the TV cameras come too. Politician X takes off his tie, puts an anorak on (a cloth cap would look too obvious and besides, an anorak serves two functions at once: it draws attention away from his Savile Row suit and genuinely offers some extra protection against the biting wind) and makes a half-hearted attempt to drop his aitches and flatten his vowels. So far so good. He's just about got away with it when he goes and does something really stupid – like saying (*à la* Peter Mandelson) that he'll have some of that delicious guacamole dip to go with his battered fish. Trouble is, he was pointing at the mushy peas. It may be an urban legend, but I enjoy it all the same.

“ *I know lots of people from London who have never been north. I actually had one person one time, albeit she was an old lady, but this is the truth, she once said to me: 'Do I need a passport to come to Birmingham?'* ***Noddy Holder***

Poor intelligence (in both senses of the word) is one thing, but what gets me is that people down south seem to wear their ignorance about the North with pride. They talk of 'the provinces' in a way that relegates us to some sort of undeveloped hinterland. They think we're stuck in the

Dark Ages – literally, since we're still waiting for our street lighting. Either that or they talk about 'the country'. 'Oh, I'm in "the country" this weekend,' they bray. And while this implies that they're not in London it doesn't usually mean they're in the real countryside, like the Fens or Snowdonia. No, it means they're at their second home a few miles up the motorway in Oxfordshire or Gloucestershire. The only consolation for us northerners is that it will have taken them about four hours just to get within spitting distance of the M40 or the M4 on a Friday evening after work, so by the time they do get to Brightwell-cum-Sotwell or Tetbury, the local pub will have stopped serving food.

Southerners act as if the North is one vast industrial wasteland, a wretched, godforsaken place. I blame William Blake. He was a Londoner and he's the one that started all these nasty rumours with his talk of 'dark, satanic mills' – inspired, if that's the right word, by the Leeds woolen mills, which employed an astonishing 10,000 people at the time when Blake wrote his poem, and exploited children horribly. They weren't even allowed to stop work to go to the toilet. And all the other southerners believe him. 'It's grim up north,' they say. For them there are only two words that could possibly follow 'grim' and the other one is 'reaper'.

That string of mill towns that seems to run one end to the other in Lancashire, I don't know what you do with those. We can't regenerate them. Are they worth regenerating? I think the most one could hope for is that we have another plague, another bout of Russian flu, that depletes the population by 20 million and then we could demolish all those places. **Brian Sewell**

I've spent a bit of time up north, doing television and book signings, and it's another world. It's not even another world, it's another planet. These people are from another planet. They don't realize it, bless them, they think they are normal and we're not. They are so odd that they don't even know they are odd. They talk very strangely, they dress extremely strangely and they serve the most ridiculous food. But they are very good-hearted, which is the most important thing of all, but beyond that, you know, they are from outer space somewhere. ***Michael Winner***

Why are southerners like this? My theory is that it makes them feel better to slag us off in the North. In particular, it makes them feel better about all those frustrations that living in the South entails, like the fact that:

- It takes them 20 minutes to walk from their house to their car and then another 40 minutes to drive to the end of their road
- They can't get to work on the Tube in the rush hour without having their nose rubbed into someone else's armpit – every day, twice a day
- They have to pay a quarter of a million for a flat the size of a rabbit hutch in an outer suburb, like Ponders End
- Paying the mortgage and council tax on their oversized broom cupboard will gobble up around 50% of their hard-earned income – for the next 25 years
- They will never be able to find a decent kitchen fitter/plumber/central heating engineer/electrician/painter and decorator/drain unblocker …
- Their children will never get into their school of first choice unless they go private.

❝ *I have no favourite place in the North, I go to the North unwillingly now. There was once a sense of an adventure in going to the North but not any more, it's a trial. I can't think of any reason for going to Newcastle unless you have to. I think that has been the situation for donkey's years. You wouldn't say, 'Let's have a dirty weekend in Newcastle' and get on a train at King's Cross. It's simply not part of the imaginary diversion, is it?* **Brian Sewell**

We've got news for you, Brian. Newcastle is *exactly* the sort of place you go to for a dirty weekend, it is full of people on the party rampage (they're not *all* sicking up in the street). In fact, in recent years Newcastle has regularly been voted one of the top ten party cities in the world. They fill an amazing 5000 hotel rooms with visitors most weekends – they're probably all tucked up with a good book by 10pm. Yes, right.

Regeneration

The North is fast catching up economically – for instance, the number of million-pound houses in the northeast has tripled during the last two years. The regeneration that has begun in the North has transformed many cities into unrecognizably cool and elegant places. Look at the two harbour photos opposite – Hartlepool (top) is looking as good as Cannes these days.

So the North is changing. The beaches are cleaner, the air fresher, the landscape altogether more graceful. You'd be lucky to find a slag heap anywhere in the North now unless it was part of a living history museum.

The new north has become trendy, with its universities attracting more than their fair share of posh kids from down south, many from public schools. They come for the night life and the cheaper cost of living, never mind the quality of the education. When I go to Tesco's in Jesmond (the middle of Newcastle's studentland) these days, I am bombarded by shrilling Piers and Giles and Sophie from Marlborough or

Ealing flaunting their winter tans and parking their ridiculously expensive cars while speaking loudly to each other on their top-of-the-range mobiles about how Daddy has just bought them a new flat 'as an investment' so they can make a bit of money renting out rooms to all their friends.

By the time I got to university in Leeds in the late Seventies, Britain was already starting to open up. People were moving around more, northerners to the South and southerners to the North, and it meant learning at first hand about how the other half lived. I think this was a good thing in general, but in a way it has made the whole North–South divide issue a lot more complicated.

It would be nice to think that, while we're not wearing

clogs any more, we could at least hang on to the best bits of our culture and traditional way of life. Because the North *is* another country, you know, and we *do* do things differently up here. But I can feel it all slipping away. Things are evening out between the North and the South and it is not necessarily a good thing. We don't want to be invaded and that is what is beginning to happen. Do we really want to exchange a good, strong cup of English tea for a skinny frappuccino? Are we to say goodbye to pies and black pudding and pints of best Yorkshire bitter, and instead live off sun-dried tomatoes from Italy and lager brewed in Prague?

CHAPTER TWO

Personality Differences

Everyone knows what the northern stereotype is. Andy Capp and his wife Florrie, basically. You know the sort of thing. Northern man wears a flat cap, races pigeons, smokes Woodbines/Capstan full strength, has a whippet, keeps a ferret up his trousers and likes a night out with the lads on the toon. Northern woman doesn't believe in wearing tights, wears earrings the size of hubcaps, travels by coach and makes a chicken last a fortnight. She also

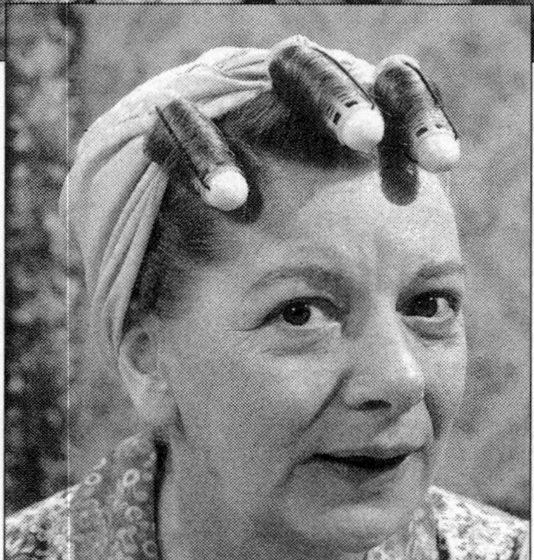

Flat caps (above) – the lasting image of northern men.

Television characters reinforce old ideas about northerners, especially if they were as lovable as *Coronation Street*'s Hilda Ogden (Jean Alexander, left).

likes a night out with the lads on the toon. But is it any wonder that people in the South get the wrong impression about northerners when everything on the telly just reinforces all these stereotypes?

But are northern people different to southerners? And if so, how exactly?

You Were Lucky; We Lived in a Paper Bag

The Monty Python team went a bit over the top with their marvellous Four Yorkshiremen sketches, what with their competitive poverty boasts and making out that life was so tough you were lucky if you got a paper bag or a cardboard box to live in, probably in the middle of the road … but like most comedy there is some truth behind it. And it's certainly true that in the past people in the North have had it hard: they've had to make a loaf of bread last a week; they've had to live with a washhouse in the yard; they've had to take turns taking out the bitty bucket on a perishing January morning; they've had to risk their health down the pit or in the steel foundry; they've had to save coins for the electricity meter; they've had to put a pound a week away towards the Christmas fund; and, more importantly, they've had to watch all their jobs disappear down the pan.

Having to overcome this sort of hardship probably means that you don't have time for idle, pretentious chit-chat. Northerners like to come to the point and get on with telling it like it is. We are traditionally direct, we know what's what. Which is probably why we need so many bouncers … and that's outside just about any establishment bar primary schools, not just the nightclubs.

I think you'll get much more straight talk from outside London than inside London. I don't know why, but I like people who will call a spade a spade and be honest with you ... there's no fannying around with a lot of verbal diarrhoea.
Carol Smillie

Being less susceptible to bullshit means that northerners are less likely to fall for stupid southern trends such as feng shui, personal trainers or life coaches. And the other thing northerners distinctly disapprove of, apart from pussyfooting around, is showing off. That's not to say that northerners aren't a proud race but we can't abide people who constantly boast about what they've achieved and flaunt it for all to see.

Brains Versus Brawn

Despite the fact that sometimes people up north are thought of as big on brawn rather than brains – or as the old proverb goes: 'Yorkshire born and Yorkshire bred, strong in the arm but weak in the head' – we can claim responsibility for an awesome list of inventions. So while the southerners are swanning around the place, flicking their hair back a lot and throwing their weight around, they would do well to bear this in mind. In fact, it could usefully be pasted up as a slogan in poster form on huge hoardings in and around the nation's capital, especially in Westminster. Here are a few examples of some of the things that owe their origins to the North.

The atom was first split by *Ernest Rutherford*, in Manchester in 1911.
The first computer was developed by *Tom Kilburn* and

Fred Williams, also in Manchester, in 1948.

The first spinning wheel, the first passenger train, the first true factory system and the first Rolls Royce all came from the North.

Steam locomotives were invented by *George Stephenson.*

TV was invented by *John Logie Baird.*

The first electric light bulb was invented by *Joseph Swan* from Sunderland, who also established the world's first electric light bulb factory, in Benwell in Newcastle in 1881. He also invented an electric battery, artificial silk and bromide photography. The first home lit by electric light was at Cragside – powered by the world's first hydroelectric power supply. The first streetlamps were put up in Mosely Street in Newcastle.

A type of rubberized cloth was invented by a Scottish chemist, *Charles Macintosh* (Mac the mac), in 1823, which was made into waterproof coats so that Scotsmen could keep their kilts dry.

The trusty thermos flask was the brain child of *James Dewar*, Scottish chemist and physicist, in 1892.

The world's first steam turbine was patented by *Charles Algernon Parsons*, in Newcastle in 1884.

Catseyes were invented by *Percy Shaw*, a road mender from Halifax, in 1890.

The Little Nipper mousetrap was patented by *James Henry Atkinson* of Leeds in 1899.

The first vacuum cleaner was invented by the Scot *Hubert Cecil Booth* in 1901.

Of course, no one's foolish enough to pretend that the South didn't contribute something to scientific and social progress. They invented Brentford Nylons for a start.

Arrogance

Surprisingly, some southerners feel that it's the northerners that are arrogant and stuck up rather than the other way round. They think we are deeply resentful and envious of what they have down south.

" *People who live in the North have an extraordinarily arrogant attitude towards those who live in the South and they make it perfectly clear that they despise us soft and silly southerners. It's deep-rooted, it is not a new phenomenon. The obvious historical roots lie with the power of the North in the industrial revolution and I think what you see now is a deep resentment, it's a kind of folk memory of what the North once was and isn't now, and it's all our fault down in the South for draining away the resources. I would argue that the North has become steadily more provincial in my lifetime, but where once it had a sort of metropolitan pride, in places like York and Newcastle, that somehow managed to disappear, and what replaced it was a kind of disgruntled envy of what was happening in the South.*
Brian Sewell

They get us so wrong, sometimes, don't they? We don't envy their traffic jams and their congestion charges and polluted air and nasty crowded streets and horrid long hours spent at their computers. We certainly don't want to emulate them. No, we want to retain our own culture and traditions. We want to make our own decisions for the future and, crucially, we want to be as wealthy and powerful as they are in the South. There's nothing wrong with that, is there?

Friendliness and Helpfulness

One difference that even your average southerner will acknowledge is that people in the North are infinitely more friendly and helpful towards one another than they are down south. People in the South are simply too preoccupied most of the time. As someone in Oxfordshire once said to the people who had recently moved in next door to them: 'We're sorry but we don't really "do" neighbours.'

In London you can live next door to people, I am told, for years and not exchange two words or one cup of sugar and I think that kind of thing comes from impersonality. People don't like to form close relationships and they are nervous of each other and if they are in contact they have got little antennae, southerners, that are kind of assessing the socio-economic status of the person: he is middle class, I can talk to him; he's upper class; he's a grovelling Cockney, or he is working class, I can kick him and be contemptuous; he's a northerner, I can freeze him out altogether. ***Austin Mitchell***

Niceness is a word that is suddenly very unfashionable but in the North we can still appreciate it.

Fred Dibnah sums up the northern man and if I could end my life and be like Fred Dibnah I'd be really, really happy. What's wrong with nice? People in the South hate that word 'nice' but the North is nice. And people are nice. ***Wayne Hemingway***

People down south are too busy with their laptops and their BlackBerrys and their spreadsheets to be nice to anyone who can't help them broker a deal. In the North we talk to one another in shops and queues, we say 'good morning' and even 'thank you' to the driver when we get off the bus, as I saw in Leeds the other day … up here we go in for all manner of small courtesies. And it is this civility that enriches our quality of life. Mind you, we can overdo it sometimes.

My mum's a bit like that, you know, she's very keen to talk to anyone in any queue, anywhere she's got to wait for more than about 10 to 15 seconds. She'll strike up a conversation with the person next to her. I've seen people take to this very kindly and I've seen people look at her a bit like, 'Who are you talking to? I don't know you.' ***Mark Radcliffe***

I think we're warmer, nicer people generally ... my friend rang up her bank manager when she was very jet-lagged, and she always ends every conversation with 'love you, love you' to the people she loves, and she means it. And she said it to her bank manager. 'I'll come around with the forms signed for the £50,000 loan,' she said. 'Thank you very much. Love you.' That was a bit embarrassing, another example of an over-friendly northerner.
Kate Robbins

Of course, people down south disagree, so we thought we'd put it to the test. Plonk ourselves in the middle of a busy shopping centre up north and ask as many people as possible to tell us directions to somewhere quite a way away, somewhere that would involve a lot of complicated geography … and yes, as you would expect, people were very helpful. They invariably stopped and went through it, once, twice or even three times. Some people stopped other people to enlist more help if they were unsure and some people put their bags down and conferred with friends before coming up with the best (though arguably the most complicated) set of directions.

Your author pretending to need directions (above). Guess where I got the brush-off and where I was given a helping hand from some lovely lasses.

Out of the 20 people we spoke to, an astonishing 19 stopped to help, despite the fact that we held everyone up for as long as we possibly could without getting punched on the nose. One woman embarked on such a long explanation she is probably still there now, going through different variations of the ways I could get to the dental hospital.

We did the same experiment down south and, as we expected, of the 20 people I stopped more than half simply brushed past me and looked fed up and annoyed at being asked at all. A mere eight people were prepared to stop for a few minutes and explain. Told you so.

Northerners are certainly more willing to stop and chat and give of their time and of themselves. I think if you stopped and asked directions in London – I mean, nine times out of ten you wouldn't get a Londoner anyway, you'd probably get someone from some other part of the country or the world – they probably would either not want to stop because you might be a bit iffy or they haven't got time. Whereas I've often seen or done it myself in Glasgow, stopped and said, 'Oh, follow me, because I'm going that way.' ***Carol Smillie***

I'd been living in London and I'd never been to Manchester or this area before and I got a job at Oldham Rep. I came up and I got off the train and I was lost so I went up to someone in the street and stopped them and asked if they could tell me where the theatre was. And they said, 'Oh yes, love' and this person walked me down there. I couldn't get over it, I almost burst into tears. From then on it was, 'Yes love, what do you want?' and all that. There was a very overt warmth and friendliness.
William Roache

Look at the average bus stop for example: in the North everyone will be chatting and exchanging news about the weather and the fact that the wind isn't quite as sharp, and asking how long the others have been waiting. Then look at one in London: everyone's plugged into their iPods or their phones, no one is even looking at anyone else, and they generally look wretchedly unhappy and unfriendly. You could almost feel sorry for them, they look so fed up.

Down south nobody says 'please' or 'thank you'. I've noticed that getting off a bus. I always say, well, I used to say, 'thank you' or 'hello'. Nobody says that getting on and off a bus in London. I used to say 'bye' when I left a shop, and everybody turned round in London, it was a bit like The Exorcist. *Heads would spin.* ***Shobna Gulati***

Not that everyone agrees, of course.

Friendlier? The North as friendly? Well, if the North began in Birmingham I would say that it is the most unfriendly city in the world. I have recently been in other cities, indeed throughout my life I've been in other cities, and I cannot say that I feel welcomed in the North, ever. No, no. You are a different animal, you are strange, they are suspicious. ***Brian Sewell***

In the North, if someone keeled over on the pavement with a heart attack, a passer-by would drop everything to help. Well, OK, not if they'd had 25 lagers and a packet of crisps on a Friday night, but then they wouldn't be a lot of help in an emergency in that state, would they? And what would a sober southerner do? They would hesitate, maybe look at their watch, then hope that a northerner comes along.

If I drop down in the street with some kind of attack or whatever in London, would anyone bother about me, other than the fact that they maybe knew my face? But if I was just anybody falling over in the street in London you might think 'ugh'. But in Glasgow they'd pick you up and look after you. I think they would; you'd have a good chat. ***Carol Smillie***

But think on: one day, when you are old and frail, when you've dropped your shopping bag, or tripped over a paving stone, or someone has mugged you, you will need some help. And maybe you will have to ask a stranger for that help. If it happens to me, and it's bound to happen because one way or another it will happens to us all, then I'd like to be in the North, please. Not in the South; no, definitely not in the South.

The Work Ethic

People in the South are on the whole too busy with their careers and promotion prospects to think about much else. What is it with them down there? Do they ever stop working? You have to feel a bit sorry for them, really. Do they ever take a break from their spreadsheets and sales targets? They need to lighten up and live a little. They want to come up north, where we knock off at 4 o'clock on a Friday and go straight down the boozer. The hooter goes off at the factory and the workers stream out of the gates and that's it for the day. They don't take their work home with them. Well, they couldn't do that exactly and OK, they don't have the most stimulating (or these days the most secure) jobs in the world, but they are able to go home and relax. Whereas down south people never seem to switch off. And they don't just worry about work. They seem to be neurotic about every little thing.

“ *We don't get so hysterical about the scaremongers. Every day you turn on the television and it's this report and that report about the dangers of salt or fat or sunbeds. And northerners think, 'Oh well, you know, I'm only here once, I might as well enjoy myself, and if it means having brown legs then I'm going to have brown legs.' 'Cos they won't wear tights, you know. In London, as soon as it hits below 19 degrees all the women think 'Black tights,' while the northern women think, 'No, another sunbed, that will see me through.'* **Jenny Eclair**

Shouting Nutcases

Less friendly is one thing, but in the South they also have more than their fair share of nutcases, or as my mother would say, people who have 'the screaming ab-dabs'. We've all seen them: the religious fanatics, the weirdos, the drunks. London is full of them. I notice that the man who stands at the entrance to Oxford Circus tube station has now traded his old-fashioned megaphone in for a fully fledged PA system, which means he's forcing an even larger number of poor sods on their way home from work to listen to his rantings.

I do think that there is a cultural difference in how people are and maybe that is 'cos London is just a disparate mass of transient people linked by a tube network. People don't make eye contact. And the only person who'll ever speak to you in the street is a shouting nutcase, of which London has a monopoly. Shouting nutcases gravitate to London. The shouting nutcases of the world gravitate to London. ***Stuart Maconie***

If you want to freak the hell out of anyone in London, just go on the Tube and say 'good morning'.
Stephen Tompkinson

If you do have to live in London, the only way to cope with it is to do what everyone else there does: never look a fellow human being straight in the eye. At all. Ever. Or you will be forced into conversation with a nutcase. And this poor soul may turn out to be a stalker or a serial killer rather than someone who has simply lost the plot. Paranoia rules and you'd better get used to it.

The London Underground, where you can ride around all day and never speak to a soul.

I remember coming down south for the first time and being really stunned when people walked past you in the street and didn't even meet your eye, never mind say hello to you. They'd look at the ground and they'd look miserable as sin.
Alan Titchmarsh

Sex Appeal

So we're friendlier, easier to deal with, more straightforward, happier, but more to the point, apparently we have more sex appeal. Yes, more sex appeal. People in the North simply ooze sexual attraction, literally in fact because so much of their flesh seems to be on show, despite the perishing weather. Just a bit of de-icer on as aftershave or perfume, and they're off.

When they're training the SAS ... never mind all that, just come to Liverpool, Merseyside in winter and see how our girls are dressed. They've got their little one-piece thing and the short skirt, and they'll be out there – hail, rain, snow, blizzards or whatever – looking fine in their little skimpy outfits and not even feeling the cold. The SAS couldn't do that. ***Louis Emerick***

You go to the North of England on a Friday or Saturday night and see the women there. They don't wear any clothes, you see what's on offer. They can look glamorous for about £15, it's brilliant. I tell you what, next time they want to do an expedition to the North Pole, don't send huskies, just send loads of women from Liverpool. Just round them up on a night out at some big hen party, strap them up - they might think it's a bit kinky at first - strap them up, crack them with a whip, off they go. They can stand the cold, no problem. ***Justin Moorhouse***

Sexy women, yes, but what about northern men? How sexy are they? Rab C Nesbitt, Ricky Tomlinson in *The Royle Family*, Peter Stringfellow, mmmm – well they've moved on from the Keegan perm, but it would take more than a couple of gays on the telly to get your average northern bloke into a pair of chinos and into using some hair mousse. But northern men do have a rugged sort of appeal, as long as they leave off the string vests, obviously. And some of us might worry about a squabble for the hair-dryer in the morning if you were to cosy up with Hugh Grant and co.

Regional Variations

It would be a mistake to assume that all northerners are the same. Those of us who live in the North are well aware of regional differences. Indeed, there are some of us who still remember the Wars of the Roses. Mrs Gaskell (born in London, raised in Knutsford, educated in Stratford-upon-Avon, started married life in Manchester) certainly appreciated the historical and cultural significance of the Lancashire–Yorkshire divide. When she went to Haworth in the West Riding to do some research for her *Life of Charlotte Brontë* in the 1850s she observed:

'Even an inhabitant of the neighbouring county of Lancaster is struck by the peculiar force of character which the Yorkshiremen display. This makes them interesting as a race; while, at the same time, as individuals, the remarkable degree of self-sufficiency they possess gives them an air of independence rather apt to repel a stranger … Indeed, there is little display of any of the amenities of life among this wild, rough population. Their accost is curt; their accent and tone of speech blunt and harsh. Some-

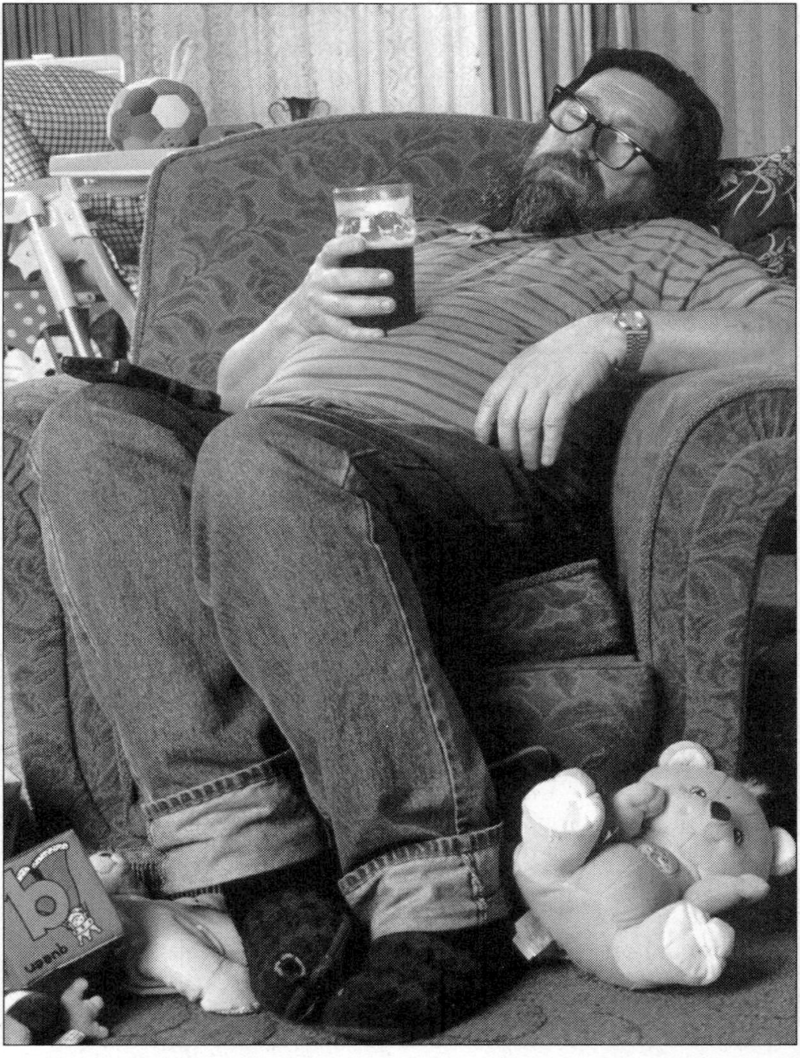

Oozing sex appeal – Ricky Tomlinson as Jim Royle.

thing of this may, probably, be attributed to the freedom of mountain air and of isolated hillside life; something be derived from their rough Norse ancestry.'

There may be one or two southerners who can tell the difference between a Geordie and a Glaswegian and some of them might even be able to identify a Liverpudlian. Can there be a member of any tribe in the whole country that is less vilified than the typical Scouser? You know the type of thing – gobby, wisecracking, a bit of dodgy dealing and living off the social. Brilliant comic that he is, Harry Enfield didn't do much for their shell-suited image. But then he is a southerner. And it's an image that is still very much alive.

Liverpudlian man, as seen by Harry Enfield and most southerners – gobby, wisecracking, dodgy-dealing, perm-headed Scousers.

Even Alan Bennett … you would expect him to be fair-minded, wouldn't you? But I suppose, being a typical Yorkshireman, he has an ingrained mistrust of anything from the other side of the Pennines, especially Liverpool.

I have come to dislike Liverpool. Robert Ross said that Dorsetshire rustics, after Hardy, had the insolence of the artist's model, and so it is with Liverpudlians. They have figured in too many plays and have a cockiness that comes from being told too often that they and their city are special. The accent doesn't help. There is a rising inflection in it, particularly at the end of a sentence, that gives even the most formal exchange a built-in air of grievance. They all have the chat, and it laces every casual encounter, everybody wanting to do you their little verbal dance.

ALAN BENNETT: *Writing Home*

There's No Place ...

An awful lot of us northerners are expats now. We no longer live and work in the area where we were born and grew up. And the thing about expats, whether they are Londoners living on the Costas or northerners living in London, is that they are always yearning for the motherland and the culture they have left behind. Expats everywhere seek each other out and then they huddle together and cling to their shared heritage.

" *My parents moved south and became more northern. I couldn't understand my mum when I phoned her up. The next time I spoke to her she put on this strange, 'Aye, 'appen I'll be ringing you next' voice. Mum, what're you doing? They'd changed, they'd started making raids to the north of England to buy their favourite kind of bread and coming back and freezing it. They have bread in Bristol, it's still there, it's still the same, but they became more proud of where they were from. I think it's probably like when the expats go and live on the Costa del Sol and they start flying the Union Jack, even though they hate Britain. It's probably the same with the North. When they're in London they have this kinship, don't they? It's like the Aussies all get together and the South Africans. Perhaps they should have clubs in London where all the expat northerners hang out and eat pies and mushy peas and drink flat beer and talk about how grim it is in t'north.* ***Justin Moorhouse***

Action Stations

But sometimes you have to do more than talk, frankly, and I think it's time for some real action to bring about the downfall of all this anti-northern prejudice without actually allowing too many southerners to move into our territory. My brilliant idea is to set up a string of 'northern' theme parks. We'll have to place them along the officially acknowledged North–South borders, obviously, in order to give the southerners the impression that they have been adventurous enough to move outside their natural comfort zone for a couple of hours. The beauty of this scheme is that it's all an illusion and the southern day-trippers will be able enjoy the amazing experience of being in the North without the expense and inconvenience of travelling long distances to get there. The best bit of all is that us northerners will never need to come into contact with them – ever.

What will people be able to see in these theme parks? All the silly stereotypes they can think of and then some. Out-of-work actors and Redcoat wannabees will be hired to walk around in flat caps and clogs (and that includes the women and children) and they will clatter along the cobbled streets on their way to t'pit or t'mill. Or maybe they'll be paying a visit to t'chippy or t'pawn shop. They'll all talk funny, of course, but there'll be audiotapes and crib sheets offering the punters a full translation. Tourists will be able to visit a typical back-to-back miner's cottage with all the usual grim accoutrements and there'll be authentic recordings (Tom Courtenay would be a good choice, or Sir

Ian McKellen) of extracts from the works of D H Lawrence. Every hour on the hour they'll blast the place with freezing cold air to remind the punters that this is what the weather's like up north and closing time each day will be announced with a factory hooter that keeps sounding until they've all left.

I've just had a thought – there'd have to be an 'honorary northern' theme park for Cornwall and Devon (and Wales) too. No problem. These places are already awash with stereotypes. Stick the Wurzels on to welcome people down to the land of pixies and pasties and clotted cream. Or in the case of Wales, Aled Jones (or a cardboard cut-out of Harry Secombe?) waving a leek and singing 'Land of My Fathers'. And then Scotland would want one of their own, of course. They've got so much tartan kitsch up there they'd have a problem choosing what to leave out.

If only the southeast didn't grab all the grants, we could try and get some lottery funding to pay for it all.

CHAPTER THREE

The Weather

We all know that living in the North is infinitely more agreeable than living in the South but the North–South weather divide is a bit of an Achilles heel for us northerners. And southerners play on this. We know that when they bang on about their architecture and their restaurants and their buzzy culture they are just showing off. But when they gloat about how much better their weather is, then this really gets us mad. 'How's the frozen north?' they say. 'You've still got the heating on, oh, poor you – it must be awful for you.'

It annoys us because, let's face it, it rings true. Everything lags behind up north. When winter looks as if it might be on the way out and the spring bulbs are poking through, some smug git from the South comes on the phone. 'Daffodils, oh no,' they say. 'We've got the roses out now.' But the truth is that weather is subjective, so not everyone agrees with me.

" *I think those who think the weather's grim up north or grimmer than it is down south, it's not so any more. The day length alters and certainly you get a longer daylight down south than you do up north. And the season is shorter because of day length. But in terms of temperature it's not nearly so marked as it used to be.* ***Alan Titchmarsh***

So with all this global climate stuff going on, maybe we're going to have the last laugh. The South will become a drought-stricken desert and the North will end up with the mild Mediterranean-type weather that the south coast boasts of today. We'll probably have olive groves, and vineyards instead of off-licences, and all sorts. Actually there is a vineyard not very far from Leeds – so the changes are happening already.

The Rain it Raineth ...

A bit of bad weather and southerners are so weedy. They go to Scarborough for the weekend and instead of coming back bowled over with the magnificent beach and coastal path they use words like 'bracing', or 'blowy', or 'bleak'. Like they live on the French Riviera or something, not in Chingford! They ring you up in early March and drop into the conversation that they've had a really sunny weekend, had their morning coffee on the patio – would you believe it! You pretend it's been the same up in Yorkshire, just to take the wind out of their sails a bit, but the truth is you've been sat round the fire all day and your trousers are still drying on the Aga from walking the dog in a blizzard.
I think some of them ring up just to make you feel bad. But then silly us. It never rains in Bournemouth or Chelsea, does it?

" *I think the media does depict weather in the Midlands and the North as bad. They put their roving reporter in front of some grotty place and it always looks like it's going to rain, it always looks dull. And I think the southerners get this impression that it's always raining in the North and we never see sunlight.*
Noddy Holder

Truth is, it might be warmer by half a degree down south but the way they go on you'd think they were living on an entirely different continent – because they don't half exaggerate it. They come to stay for the weekend and demand hot-water bottles (in July) and purposely forget to bring a jumper and then ask to borrow one (or two) and wear a muffler indoors to shame you into putting the heating on. When I get a minute I'm going to sneak some live webcams into the houses of some of my friends down south and so when they call and say they are lolling on their sunbeds in the garden or setting the table for lunch outside or doing a barbecue (not even in the garage or anything) I'm going to check. Because half the time I think they make out it's about five degrees hotter than it actually is. I mean, hold on, how different can the temperature really be down south? We live in a teeny-weeny country. Ian Botham once walked from one end to the other, and he's not exactly Paula Radcliffe's build is he? So if the country's that titchy, how different can the weather really be down south?

Londoners really milk the apparent difference in our climates. You get called down to head office for a pointless meeting, you've dressed in the dark, you put your big coat on because it's perishing, and by the time you get there it's baking hot. They're all in their flip-flops with the air-conditioning on and they make you feel so stupid for being wrapped up in so many layers.

“ *I have a duvet-type coat on that goes down to my ankles that I wear a lot and I get on an early morning shuttle down to London and I wear it and I look really stupid when I get there. Everyone is in summer dresses and there's me with a bit of dribble down the side of my face because I've fallen asleep on the plane.* ***Carol Smillie***

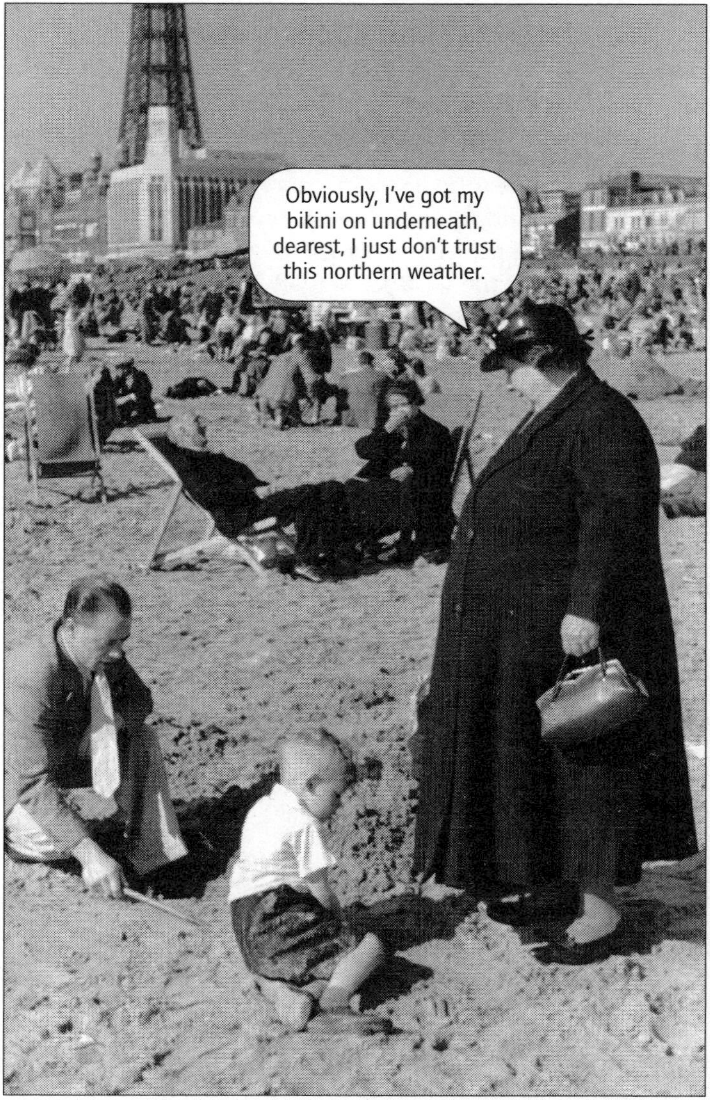
Obviously, I've got my bikini on underneath, dearest, I just don't trust this northern weather.

Of course, for the purposes of this chapter, those in the southwest (our bit of the honorary north) need to peel off … they need to peel off and make themselves a nice cup of tea because they do have slightly nicer weather in North Devon than Cumbria and Yorkshire. But at least they don't stuff it down everyone else's throats and make us feel inferior. No, Londoners and people within the M25 are, as usual, the enemy in this respect, I'm afraid.

So how does the weather actually differ from north to south? Having done some serious research, we are pleased to announce the following cheery statistics.

- Leeds has one of the driest climates in the country and gets slightly less rain than Barcelona and a lot less than Milan.
- Sheffield and Bradford each get less rain than Cannes.
- Sheffield is warmer in July than Newquay in Cornwall – well sometimes it is, although there is less call for surfboards in South Yorkshire.
- Parts of Devon get more rain than Durham and it rains more in Cornwall than it does in Manchester – mostly when us northerners are there on holiday, so we have to spend our wet afternoons in a dreary motorcycle museum or looking for a tea shop in which to shelter from the rain.
- Edinburgh has more hours of sunshine per year than Stratford-upon-Avon.
- You are more likely to have to scrape ice off your windscreen in parts of Sussex than you would in Durham.

So you see, it's not all bad up north. But to hear them talk, you'd think it never rained at all down south. However, we cannot deny that Bognor Regis on the south coast is the sunniest place in the UK. And we cannot deny that we've had a good old tinker with some of the stats in the showy-offy bit above and been a bit selective with the figures here and there, but it made you feel better, right?

And here's another interesting fact: there have only been four occasions during the last hundred Wimbledons when it hasn't rained. Even when King George V opened the Centre

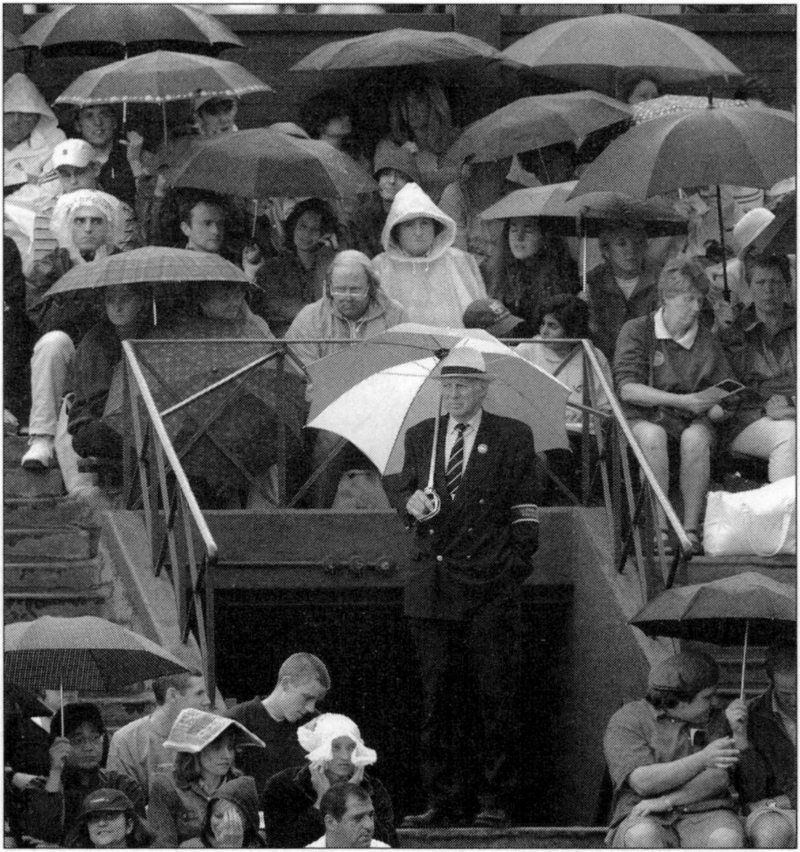

Tennis fans subjecting themselves to the annual misery of Wimbledon.

Court in 1922 there was a rain delay and it was wet every day of the championships thereafter. In fact, 96 per cent of the championships have been rained on – in 118 years of Wimbledon there have only been five that haven't seen any rain. But they don't go on about that down south, do they?

(We decided to find out what the actual differences are between the weather in the South and the North. We don't necessarily want this sort of classified information getting into enemy hands too readily, so I've tucked away the real facts at the end of this chapter. You can tear the page out in a jiffy once you've read it and it's rain-degradable, so chances are it will have self-destructed in a couple of days.)

Unfortunately, once in a while the weather in the North lets us down big time, like it did when we hosted the Commonwealth Games in Manchester in 2002. This important sporting event, the biggest this country has ever staged, was going swimmingly (well, not literally – that came later) until it was time for the closing ceremony. This was to be broadcast live on TV. And then it poured, and poured and poured. It was not just a light girly drizzle but

came down in great big sploshes. Everyone in the arena got drenched and all those smug commentators in their nice dry studios in London had a laugh at Manchester's expense. Even the Queen had to open her own umbrella – and it looked like she'd never done that before.

Baby, It's Cold Outside

It's not that we necessarily get *worse* weather in the North, we get … well, *more* weather if you see what I mean – real weather, the kind of weather that means you need to pull your bobble hat down over your ears; the kind of weather that lashes under the back door and blows the dustbins down the street; the kind of weather that means you have the windscreen wipers on fast for hours on end, that kind of weather. Nothing nancy, like a fine mist or a sprinkling of snow, but real snow, deep snow, the sort of snow that means you have to dig the car out.

In Newcastle, where I come from, it is certainly colder than it is in London but you know, I like that, I like the changes in temperature. In the summer in London, it's airless, it's hot, it's sweaty, it's debilitating. If you get a gorgeous day in the northeast in the summer, you know, blue skies, fantastic sun but there is always a breeze, it's nice. I like the weather in the North better. And you know we get snow there, you never get snow in London, it's a pathetic excuse for snow you get there. You get a bit of sleet on the road. If you are going to get snow you want snow, you want four foot of it. ***Carole Malone***

This year, in the village in which I live in the North, there was snow in mid-November, and I rejoiced in going out again and shovelling snow. I mean, I was back doing real things in the real world, I was shovelling snow in November, and that's slightly crazy but it's also an indication of our pride at being up there. Well, London comes to a standstill if there's two inches of snow. I mean, I've seen London paralyzed by what I would regard in the north of England as a flurry. London isn't used to this sort of thing and London takes it very hard. ***Roy Hattersley***

Weather up north isn't something you natter about idly when you're running out of conversation at the school gates. It is rarely just OK, it's either blowing a gale and raining so hard it gets inside your wellies or cold enough to freeze the proverbial monkey's. In the North, weather is really, really important. And because it's such a roller coaster up here, we're always grateful even if it's only halfway good. 'The wind's not so bad today,' people will say cheerily, or 'Nice drying day,' thankful for a bit of sun in spite of the sharp wind. And when it's really sunny everyone scampers around, organizing last-minute barbecues and sitting on the front step peeling potatoes. We don't expect good weather, so when it does happen we are tickled pink. We should do what the Swedes do: they are determined to sit outside and eat, no matter what the weather (and they get some of the worst in Europe). Go to Stockholm and you will find that every restaurant has tables outside on the pavements all year round. They just light one of those big oil heater lamps and supply little blankets for you to put over your legs. Now that's stylish, that's pragmatic. We're descended from the Vikings up here, after all, so I like to think that we have something of the old Scandinavian spirit bred into us.

❝ *Buying a convertible anywhere in England, but particularly in the north of England ... you almost want to say to those people, 'Good for you, son.' 'Cos you know you're gonna use that car just one day of the year or so. But you're still gonna go for it. I love that, that indomitable spirit. We will not be beaten down by the elements.* ***Stuart Maconie***

“ *You go to Torquay, Blackpool or anywhere like that and you'll get tons of Scots going for the weekend. It's not even remotely sunny or warm and yet they're on that beach, they've got their vests on and they're up to there in mud. And you think, 'Bless them, they're blue, absolutely bright blue with cold, but dammit, they're on holiday,' and that's what you do on holiday.* ***Carol Smillie***

And there are more private swimming pools installed in the North than in the South too, which is further proof – if further proof is needed – that people up north neither feel the cold nor are put off by a spot of bad weather.

Because the sun doesn't shine in the North every day, like it does in Los Angeles, when it does happen it turns us into over-enthusiastic children. We sit on the beach until it turns us beetroot and we stay behind our windbreakers until the sun's gone down and the tide's lapping at our toes. We certainly make the most of it.

There are some advantages to this climate of ours up here. You can pretty much wear the same wardrobe all year round. You might leave off the thermal long johns for a couple of days in August but you can save a fortune on summer frocks. People up north tend to buy just the one to last a lifetime. They're so old they've got bust darts and patch pockets and look like something out of *I Love Lucy*.

And anyway, why is warmer always better? Cold and crispy is nice – nice clear blue skies and a cool wind is nice. Up in the North we like that. Honest, we do like that.

Up north we're built for the weather, biologically designed to withstand sub-arctic temperatures while still having a good time. We officially don't feel the cold, especially when we've had a few Bacardi Breezers … why else would we go out on the toon in our bikinis? And the reason why we don't feel the cold like the namby-pambies down south is because we've been sitting in freezing cold football stadiums for years and this has genetically modified us into thinking that jumpers and coats are for wusses.

“ *I once went to see Arsenal play Sunderland on a freezing December day at Highbury and it was hilarious watching the two ends of the ground. There was a bunch of blokes in car coats and balaclavas and then down the other end there was, like, 25,000 blokes or something like that in white cap-sleeve T-shirts going, 'Call this cold? I'm thinking of taking me shirt off.'*
Stuart Maconie

I think there's no doubt that northerners and southerners perceive the weather in a different way. Northerners are taught to tolerate the cold weather from birth. When I was growing up my mother and all the other northern mothers were obsessed with fresh air. They were always opening the windows, airing the beds and putting their babies out in the garden in their prams. We were like the geraniums that my dad used to shuffle between the greenhouse and the garden in the spring to get them used to the conditions outside until it was warm enough for them to cope unaided. It was a ritual that seemed unspeakably tedious to me when I was a teenager but I can see the point of it now. And that's what northern mothers were doing to their children: hardening them off like tender plants until they were tough enough to manage on their own.

Out in the garden, never mind the temperature – northerners take advantage of the tiniest bit of sunshine.

Londoners have their own microclimate to contend with, most notably the foul humidity they are likely to encounter on the Tube. Southern mothers deal with this by strapping their toddlers into their buggies and pushing them through the muggy streets of Peckham and Brixton in order to prepare them for the Piccadilly Line in adult life. That's how Londoners manage to survive the underground in temperatures that would fry an egg on your *Evening Standard.* But give them a couple of inches of snow and it's newsflash time – they all take the day off work and ponce about with silly little shovels like big girls' blouses.

When I moved to London, it was quite interesting, people's attitude to a bit of cold. I remember one day, the first winter I was there, and there was a smattering of snow on the ground, and honestly, there were people coming into work dressed as if they had just done the Eiger or something, you know, hiking boots and big sheepskin hats, like Nanook of the North. And they'd come in on the bloody Tube! ***Mark Radcliffe***

And Here Is the Weather Forecast

Weather reports don't help. They just fuel our anger and frustration. For a start, weather reports are vitally important if you live in the North, they're not just the bit you casually watch at the end of the news while you're flicking channels. Which is why it is particularly infuriating that most of their information and emphasis is on detailed reports of – guess where? – London and the southeast. Here is a typical weather report:

> *It'll start off cloudy in Hammersmith, then you might get a proper shower or two as far out as Slough, and then by lunchtime it should be really sunny in Hampshire, but if you live in the East End or you're working in the City, you might want to take your lunch early, as it will soon cloud over, and by 3 o'clock it will be raining everywhere.* [Everywhere in London is what they mean.] *Oh ... and the North will have heavy rain and high winds later.*

❝ *A few years back I sat watching Penny Tranter or Rob McElwee or someone with a big, smiling face, pointing to that big, fat, smug, orange sun logo over London and saying it was going to be the best weekend since records began. 'Do enjoy yourself, and if you're getting out and about, do remember to put some sun cream on, particularly if you've got little kids with you.' And I was in a cottage in the Lake District, and I looked out of the window and men with sandbags were trying to stop the river from flooding the house. And it was like a sick joke. It was pissing down in the whole north of England. We were up to our necks in*

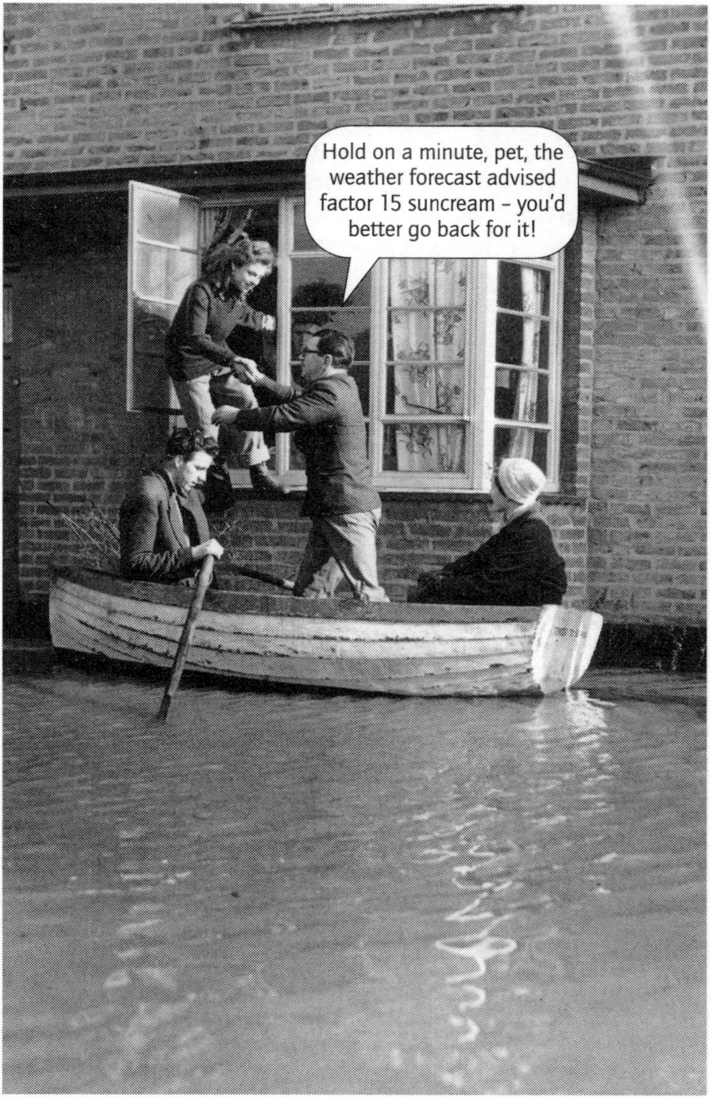
Hold on a minute, pet, the weather forecast advised factor 15 suncream – you'd better go back for it!

water. But it was sunny in London, so hey, that's all right, then.
Stuart Maconie

And if it is blowing a gale up north in July, and I have to admit, it does happen, the weather forecasters seem to be entirely unsympathetic, like living up north means that you have to take that sort of thing in your stride, so pull yourselves together. Of course, if they get a bit of wind down south then the whole world gets to hear about it.

“ *Why is it when they have a weather forecast for the whole country, there is always a great big black cloud over the North because they just expect that the weather is going to be crap? So if the South is going to get half an inch of rain the weather forecaster goes, 'Wrap up warm and put your galoshes on'. In the North, they don't pander to you at all. There is no sympathy because they just assume that you are used to it and that you can deal with it. If there is a puddle in Putney it's news.*
Carole Malone

The BBC fuelled our anger good and proper when it brought in the 3-D weather map that was tilted to favour the South – the North looked like it was on the edge of the world, literally at the end of beyond. So many of us complained that they changed it, but in my opinion, all that whizzing around from the North to the South makes me dizzy. I was happy with the nice, non-swanky, straightforward one with all the isobars and a weatherman with a long, pointy stick. But there we are.

“ *When you look at the weather forecast I think it is still based very much on what is happening in the south of England. I mean, if it snows in Scotland, oh well, that's Scotland, 'cos it always snows in Scotland. Everyone in the south of England thinks that Scotland just grinds to a halt for six months of the year 'cos it's just iced over like a glacier has come down and covered it, and they sort of expect that. And then you get a few road closures up here or whatever, but when snow hits the south of England, oh my God, it's the first story on the news, you know. It's just ridiculous.* ***Mark Radcliffe***

Given the choice … well, you can guess what I would prefer. Give me the fresh air option any day. You don't get much of that down south. Even on the white cliffs of Dover, with a sea breeze tousling your hair, it's still not what I would call fresh air. Not enough to give you a rosy-cheeked glow and send you off to sleep the minute your head hits the pillow; not enough to make you feel better about your life or think a problem through. No, you need some good proper northern fresh air for that.

The way we northerners cope with the weather is to ignore it. It's the only way. We go out on the town in our underwear in near Arctic temperatures, get drunk, hunt in packs, have a good time getting legless, and then stumble into the Indian for a vindaloo to warm up. There you are. All love bites and sick, that's us. What's a good night out if you don't call the emergency services? That's what we say.

This is the data I mentioned on page 76.

According to the Met Office these are the climatic differences between the South and the North of England averaged out over the last 30 years.

	NORTH	SOUTH
temperature	12.1°C	13.6°C
rainfall	944.5 mm	781.5 mm
days of rain	142.3	125.3
hours of sunshine	1348.6	1515

The warmest place in the UK is the Isles of Scilly, with an average mean temperature of 14°C. But Jersey claims to be the warmest too, and so does Eastbourne and so does Bognor, so they'll just have to fight it out while we do something more interesting. The coldest place is Braemar in the Grampians, Scotland, with an average mean (and I do mean mean) temperature of 6.5°C.

If you want reliable summer heat, then the best place to go is the southwest, in the shelter of Dartmoor – it's not called the English Riviera for nothing. The prize for the wettest place goes either to the Lake District or just over the border to the southwest of Scotland. It is often a dead heat between the two regions but in 2004 the honour went to Seathwaite near Borrowdale in Cumbria, with an impressive 3300 mm (130 inches) for the year. The wettest major city in the UK is Swansea. This may come as a surprise to some of you, especially in Manchester, but presumably not if you live in South Wales.

CHAPTER FOUR

Accents and Regional Dialects

There are two opposing schools of thought when it comes to regional accents: one is that they are more evident than ever before and the other is that they are becoming obsolete and so are being sold at car-boot sales.

It's Not What You Say ...

According to a study on regional accents that the BBC carried out in 2005, three quarters of the 50,000 people in the UK that they surveyed felt that they now heard a lot more accents in everyday life and on TV and radio than before. But accents aren't what they used to be. Back in the 1930s, photojournalist Humphrey Spender headed off to Bolton to make a record of how people lived for a study called Mass-Observation. If he'd done it today it would have been on telly, they would have called it *Big Brother* and he would have made a bob or two out of it. Anyway, he spent months recording and analyzing regional accents – trouble is, he couldn't understand a single word. 'It was like a foreign language,' he said, on a BBC documentary shown to mark the fiftieth anniversary of the project in 1987. 'I simply could not follow what they were saying.' And he wasn't kidding – he had to employ a local called Harry Gordon to act as interpreter. So I'm guessing that these days accents are relatively mild and much of our speech is homogenized, like the milk they sell at the Co-op.

Since we all watch *Coronation Street* and *Emmerdale* now, southerners are totally at home with the way people speak in Manchester or Yorkshire. But roll back to the 1970s and I bet you a phrase book would have come in handy when they watched Ena Sharples and Minnie Caldwell having a chinwag in the snug at the Rovers Return.

Don't fret, Ena, pet, they'll soon get the hang of what we're on about.

To throw some more statistics at you: 78% of people who took part in the survey said they enjoy hearing a variety of regional accents. Hence even the voice you hear when you phone National Rail Enquiries is currently that of a woman with subtle but friendly northern vowels. Clever, or what? Apparently, 72% of the British population think that they have at least a 'moderately strong' accent, 4% admit their accent is very strong and 6% claim to have no accent at all (presumably 18% didn't understand the question in the first place), which, according to the experts, is not allowed. They say there is no such thing as 'no accent'. Everyone has an accent and all accents are regional. This even applies to the upper crust who live in clusters in Chichester or Chelsea. They are the dinosaurs of the accent world and we all know what happened to the dinosaurs …

“ *I feel a bit sorry for people with posh accents these days, they sound a bit stupid. If you listen back to received pronunciation on radio and television in the 1950s and 1960s it sounds ludicrous now. Everybody has become a lot more mangled in their speech. I don't think that's a bad thing. If everybody ended up talking exactly the same that would be very dull.* ***Jenny Eclair***

While it's no longer the case that you have to sound like Celia Johnson (the upper-class heroine of *Brief Encounter*) or Richard Baker to get on in the professions, there are no prizes for guessing why British life is still dominated by people who speak a dumbed down form of 'posh'. You only have to turn on the radio or TV to see just how much southern clipped English there is out there, controlling the media and all the other corridors in the institutions of power. People who sound like Jeremy Paxman, Sarah Montague, David Dimbleby and Sue Lawley (who hails from Dudley in the West Midlands, though you'd never guess) have the kind of voices that are considered to be authoritative and politically neutral. And try walking into a magistrates' court anywhere in the country and you'll be hard pushed to find a strong regional accent on the bench.

Regional accents might have become politically correct in some circles but most of us feel that they are something

Richard Baker, the voice of BBC News from the 1950s to the 1970s.

of a hindrance if we want to get on in life. More than four in five admit to changing their accent to accommodate different situations, and according to the Azis Corporation, who did a survey in 2000, 57% of the British company directors they questioned said that regional accents are undesirable. Even today, someone who speaks the Queen's English (by which they mean southern) is likely to be more successful. They claim that the worst accents are those from Liverpool, Birmingham and the West Country. Worse than that, those same company directors admitted that when they met someone with a Scottish accent 43% saw them as successful, honest and hard-working, but only 9% had the same reaction on meeting a Liverpudlian.

The BBC survey came to pretty much the same conclusion. They found that there was a close link in people's minds between pleasantness and prestige. An Edinburgh accent scored quite highly on both counts while Liverpool and Birmingham accents were condemned as being both unpleasant to listen to and lacking in social status. So a drop of Dublin or a soupçon of Scottish is fine, but it has to be perceived as classy as well as attractive.

There appear to be two major exceptions to this pattern. Many people thought a London accent might be quite helpful career-wise but they did not find it very attractive. And conversely, the majority of respondents liked the sound of the Newcastle accent but did not think it was very prestigious or useful when job hunting. Which means that it's probably dead easy for a Cockney to get a job in Newcastle and no trouble at all for a Geordie to get laid in London. But then we knew that already.

The survey asked people whose accents they liked the best – these were the top ten most popular celebrity voices:

Sean Connery
Trevor McDonald
Terry Wogan
Hugh Grant
Moira Stuart
The Queen
Billy Connolly
Ewan McGregor
Joanna Lumley
Pierce Brosnan

It is interesting that the Scots are so well represented here and even more interesting that one of them, Billy Connolly, also appears along with the Queen in the list of voices that people most hate. It only goes to show that we feel uncomfortable with extremes, I guess. Maybe Billy and Her Majesty could spend a little time together and flatten one another's accents out. They're both partial to a hike in the heather, after all. They could be new best friends.

And here are the top ten celebrities with the least popular voices:

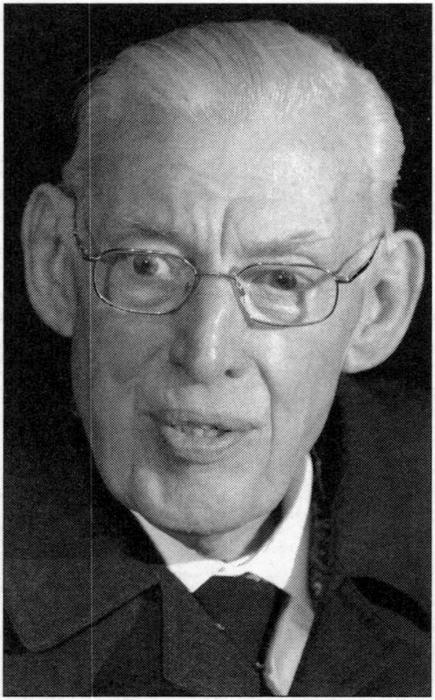

Ian Paisley
Billy Connolly
Cilla Black
Lily Savage
Jasper Carrott
Janet Street-Porter
David Beckham
The Queen
Frank Skinner
Tony Blair

My Ain Folk

It is no surprise that people in the BBC survey indicated a preference for their own regional accents. So the Scots said they loved Ewan McGregor's Perthshire accent, the English found Hugh Grant's voice attractive and the Welsh preferred listening to the actor Richard Burton and news-reader Huw Edwards. People in Northern Ireland found Terry Wogan's mellifluous tones from Limerick irresistible and this was the only group that failed to put Ian Paisley at the top of their hate list.

The accents that have been voted the sexiest, by the way, were Scottish, Irish and Geordie, and the least sexy was Birmingham. Poor old Brummies. They don't even like their own accents much: if they had the chance, 63% of people living in the West Midlands would change the way they spoke.

The thing with the Birmingham accent is that it makes people sound a bit simple, doesn't it? It's not true and it's not fair but it's a stereotype. As soon as anybody from Birmingham starts to speak, you immediately think of Crossroads and Benny. They wouldn't harm you; they're like pandas, they're like big, slow bears that want to be dynamic. But you can't be dynamic with that accent, can you? **Justin Moorhouse**

The thing about the Midlands is, it's in the middle, it's neither here nor there, and I think we feel the same about the people. I shouldn't say that because it's terribly offensive to people in Birmingham but I just hate the accent and I don't know anyone who likes it – apart from people who live there.
Carole Malone

Brad Pitt he isn't. Even after all these years, Benny from *Crossroads* (Paul Henry) is still most people's idea of a typical Brummie.

“ *The Brummie accent really is quite vile, isn't it? They're nice people but it's a pretty unattractive accent. It's very unsexy, which is really unfortunate if you happen to be from there because you can't help it.* ***Carol Smillie***

“ *I could never ever sleep with a man from Birmingham. You just couldn't do it, I'd be laughing. Even if he looked like Brad Pitt.* ***Shobna Gulati***

Could be time to open up elocution lessons in Birmingham and the Black Country. You'd clean up.

I can remember the first time I ever heard someone talk on the telly in a Brummie accent like mine. She sounded just like me and my neighbours. It was in the 1960s, on a show on the BBC called *Juke Box Jury* hosted by David Jacobs. This woman in the studio audience, Janice Nicholls, gave her verdict (on a score of one to ten) on the latest pop record and said, 'I'll give it five.' Phonetically speaking, it came out as 'Oi'll geeve eet foive' and it became her catchphrase. Because everyone had a catchphrase back then. Janice made such an impact and was so popular that they invited her to appear on the show every week after that. She put the Brummie accent on the map and in our innocence we all thought that we were now going to be trendy. After all, the Beatles had introduced the world to the Liverpool sound. Silly us. People just went on taking the mickey out of Birmingham and the way we spoke. Janice faded from public view and took her accent with her. Last thing we heard, she was working in a shoe shop in Coventry.

Why does this particular accent come in for so much stick? It's not as if it doesn't have immensely impressive credentials. For instance, why don't the actors at the RSC at Stratford deliver their lines in broad Brummie?

Shakespeare would have spoken a bit like Noddy Holder, which is marvellous. Actually that's Black Country. He would have spoken certainly like some of the people on Crossroads. And it's funny how London in particular colonizes the best bits that it wants to. So you walk down by Oxford Circus where they're selling you those postcards of people with Mohicans and Princess Diana and all the other things that we're supposed to feel fabulously proud of in Britain, like the Houses of Parliament and Buckingham Palace. I'm sure there's a picture of Shakespeare in there somewhere. But don't tell them that he's actually from Birmingham. I think he's just become part of heritage Britain now, hasn't he? **Stuart Maconie**

There's No Business Like Show Business

If there's one area of modern life where it is very much OK to have a strong regional accent it's the entertainment industry. If you want to present certain programmes on TV and radio, like reality shows, pop music or sport, it's pretty much a requirement. You wouldn't get very far as a DJ on commercial radio if you sounded like a Tory MP, would you? You'd book a comedian with a Brummie accent but would you hire a lawyer with one? And you'd automatically cast a Cockney in *EastEnders* but would you hop happily onto the operating table if the surgeon talked like Pauline Fowler?

❝ *But we'll know that the struggle has been won, brothers and sisters, when somebody who talks like me is presenting Newsnight. Or when Ant and Dec, not Ant and Dec themselves, fine men though they are, but someone who speaks like Ant and Dec is doing Horizon or whatever its modern equivalent is. There are certain accents that are not regarded as serious enough for certain jobs on telly ... even the weather.* **Stuart Maconie**

There's no doubt that if you're looking for the popular touch a northern accent offers people a way of sneaking under the radar. You now get a sort of inverted snobbery and some broadcasters are so desperate not to sound too posh or middle class that they deliberately broaden the way they speak. Can you blame them? People don't want their entertainers to remind them of their head teachers.

I think in my job having an accent helps, because, let's face it, the majority of the country is from the North. It just gives you a bit more cred. I mean, when I go into people's homes in the North, I think they think, 'OK, she's one of us,' and it's true, I am. But I think if I went in all la-di-da, they wouldn't talk to me.
Carole Malone

Another one of my bugbears: you turn on local radio and you get fools playing up their northern accents, which is really, really patronizing. ***Stuart Maconie***

Commercial Breaks

Television advertising is always a useful barometer to what's in and what's out when it comes to the way we speak. Next time the ads come on have a look at how they make use of voices, accents and regional stereotypes. What are they trying to tell us?

If it's something that's not remotely glamorous, if it's to do with baked beans, or tea, or insurance, it's a northern voice. If it's to do with flash cars or beauty or glamour, it's always a southern accent. And that really ticks me off, because I think, 'Do they imagine that nothing glamorous happens in the North?' If they are selling something that they think is for the masses, they will use a northern accent and that is really insulting, actually.
Carole Malone

Anything that would be regarded as a posh product like Ferrero Rocher or anything that's got a posh name, I don't think they'd necessarily pick on me. But I'm the down-to-earth products, you know, the products that really matter. And the products that people like. That's what they more or less go for with me. I suppose it all boils down to ... I'm common as muck ... I don't think you'd probably ask me to advertise Crystal champagne, for example. ***Noddy Holder***

And now the politicians are getting in on the act, adapting the way they speak in order to prove to the electorate that they have the common touch. They're just like the advertisers when it comes to brand imaging. Well, politics is more or less a branch of showbiz now, isn't it?

We Have Ways of Making You Talk

Would you guess from the way he speaks that Tony Blair was educated in Edinburgh and represents a constituency in the northeast of England? His accent comes across as a neutral form of received pronunciation but he occasionally lapses into a bit of London Estuary if he wants to be matey. Gordon Brown is at a distinct advantage when it comes to wowing the voters. He has a high credibility rating partly, presumably, because of his Scottish accent. You get the feeling he wouldn't bother changing it for anyone. And neither would a down-to-earth northerner like John Prescott. If anything, he probably exaggerates his accent because it suits him to stick to the broad Yorkshire he grew up with. It puts him on the right side of 'them and us' (or 'them people' as I heard him say on Radio 4 the other day) and we don't challenge him. He'd never have got away with all the gobsmacking gaffes that he has committed over the years if he sounded like he'd been to Eton.

Alan Milburn's accent fascinates me. He comes from my neck of the woods, Northumberland, and I can't help thinking that he might be playing it up a bit. I haven't met anyone else with vowels quite like his. They are more than flat, they are so flat you could post them under the door.

Things have certainly changed since Maggie's day. Mrs Thatcher, the upwardly mobile grocer's daughter from Grantham, was motivated to shed her native accent via grammar school, Oxbridge and the Conservative Party. She played by the Establishment rules for getting on in politics and ended up sounding more like a southerner than many southerners. But do you remember the time she used the dialect word 'frit' instead of 'frightened'? The media pounced on that inadvertent exposure of her northern roots like a pack of bloodthirsty foxhounds.

Talking Proper

Most people tend to poshen up their accent if they go for a job interview and a lot of us have a Sunday-best voice for when we answer the phone or talk to the doctor. We save our real accent for our family and friends. In the North, if we're nervous about the impression we are going to give by the way we speak, we get into a right flap. Show us a word with an 'a' in the middle, like 'laugh' or 'basket', or one beginning with an 'h', and we don't know which way to go. First of all we have to consider who we are talking to and then we need to take a bit of a run up to it. No wonder we sometimes mess it up good and proper.

I think what's funny is the way northerners try to correct the way they speak and get it wrong. In the work I've done over the last few years I've had to play southerners and I've had to play posh. I've had to elongate my vowels, so I'll say 'claaaaas' and 'baaath' instead of 'bath', but then you get it wrong and say, 'I was staaaanding next to Princess Aaaaane.' ***Kate Robbins***

When I started doing Gardeners' World I had a letter from a lady, and it was a serious letter. 'I've just started gardening,' she said, 'and I'm confused about this word "plant". You say "plant" and other people say "plant" as though it has an "r" in it. Can you please tell me which is correct?' I still have the letter. And I had to write back to her and say it was a regional variation. I do find it difficult, having been down south now, I'm ashamed to admit, for longer than I lived up north. I still struggle with 'bath' and 'grass'. ***Alan Titchmarsh***

Takes One to Know One

Accents and dialects are more than just the pronunciation. Northern people talk in an entirely different way.

I know instantly if my wife is talking to my mum in Wigan on the phone because she's not saying anything. Because one question will have elicited a massive response, a kind of Icelandic saga of a response that involves having to tell you about every person who's related to every person in the story. It's like a Tolkien-ish saga. You know, if you read Tolkien, it's always full of, 'Thus did Gimley, son of Gloin, descendant of Nagreb ... ' If my mum tells you a story about something that's happened in the street, it's, 'Jimmy, you know Jimmy, Jimmy one-leg, lost his eye at the foundry, used to be married to that woman who worked in the chip shop. Two kids, you know, their twins, one of them used to play for Wigan Rugby League. You do, you know them.' And so it goes back and back and back to the dawn of recorded time, like the Bible. And that's why all northern stories take an age to tell.
Stuart Maconie

Those expats who have emigrated to the South (maybe in a moment of carelessness they found themselves marrying someone from Croydon or perhaps they got themselves a job in the media) can find it hard to influence their children. They end up with kids who speak universal Estuary English with an antipodean gloss.

> *I'm saddened that my kids don't have a northern accent really, if I'm honest. It would be nice if they just had those flat vowels. But the most depressing thing now is that they've both got a slight Australian twang because they watch Neighbours. It's very worrying. I mean, where are you from? Melbourne?*
> ***Alan Titchmarsh***

These days you can buy all sorts of phrase books to help you decipher local accents – some make very entertaining reading. *Lern Yerself Scouse* is an invaluable guide, especially if you're about to go out on the piss in Liverpool on a Friday night. Most of the phrases in the book are to do with confrontation and boozing, often at the same time. Typical chapter headings are: 'Starting an Altercation' and 'How to Chat Someone up in an Alehouse'. Here are a few examples:

She gorra face like a ruptured custard
She's not very attractive.
I avent ad a road through me for a week
I am constipated.
Don't get airyated
Keep calm.
I'll ang one on yer
I'll punch you one.
Bevvied up, lushed up
Drunk.
I'll purra fluke's go on ter yer
I'll give you a blow.

Larn Yersel' Geordie is equally stereotypical in content but here the emphasis is on football, for example:

Hoositganninathematch?
How is the football game progressing?
Thebuggarswantshingin
I have the gravest doubts as to the ability of the directors of the football team.
Thordeeincanny
Our noble lads are performing successfully with their usual skill.
Whyaye
I absolutely agree, old fruit.
Morderthebee
We disagree with the referee's decision.
Yewantipackin
Apply for a transfer.

For some reason, being a Geordie is particularly cool these days, ever since Terry and Bob (James Bolam and Rodney Bewes) appeared in *The Likely Lads* and then Bolam took his full-on northeastern vowels to *When the Boat Comes In* (or *When the 'Boot' Comes In)*. Gradually, the Geordies won over the South and now you can't move for them. Like Ant and Dec, they're all over the media and a Geordie accent is very *à la mode* in places like the Groucho Club or Soho House.

By comparison, Cockney rhyming slang is rather pathetic, don't you think? Apart from anything else, most of the words and phrases seem just a bit odd rather than intriguing or witty. And some of them seem entirely inappropriate or just plain illogical. Take the following:

Schindlers/Schindler's List *pissed*
Edinburgh Fringe *minge*

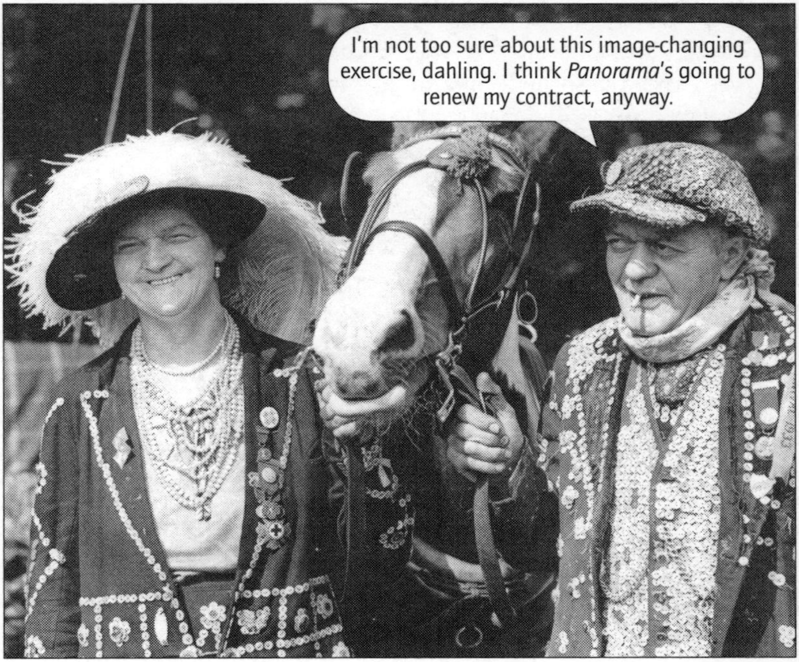

Forrest Gump *dump*
chocolate fudge *judge*
Cape of Good Hope *soap*
army and navy *gravy*
Mystic Megs *legs*

That last one is a bit dodgy, isn't it? Mystic Meg hasn't been on the telly for donkey's years. Occasionally, though, they do come up with the odd one that does tickle my fancy, like pitch and toss for 'boss' or fromage frais for 'gay'.

If you're feeling really confident you can try to decode this one:

'Allo me old china – wot say we pop round the Jack. I'll stand you a pig and you can rabbit on about your teapots. We can have some loop and Tommy and be off before the dickory hits twelve.'

Which translated means:

Hello my old mate (china plate) – what do you say we pop around to the bar (Jack Tar). I'll buy you a beer (pig's ear) and you can talk (rabbit and pork) about your kids (teapot lids). We can have some soup (loop de loop) and supper (Tommy Tucker) and be gone before the clock (hickory dickory dock) strikes twelve.

Northern Mystique

I love the music of northern accents, the way they dance around. They are so much more expressive than bland middle-class English. People up north can communicate in different ways. Sometimes they spin out a tale with poetic meanderings and other times they have so much inner energy you think they're going to spontaneously combust. If all their normal jobs were to disappear tomorrow, northerners would have no trouble hiring themselves out as professional storytellers … probably funded by the Arts Council. As well as having the gift of narration, northerners are quite affectionate when they speak to each other and this can add a special rhythm to what they say.

All my boyhood I was surrounded by people who called each other 'love'. I mean, steel workers paying their tuppence on the bus would say to the male bus conductor, 'I'm sorry I've no change, love.' And indeed I sometimes do it now and I have to apologize to young ladies on the phone. I say, 'OK, love,' and I say after, 'Forgive me, this is not sexism, this is not me being politically incorrect, I'm just a Yorkshireman and I would call your grandfather "love", I would call your brother "love".' It's not me being patronizing to women. 'Love' is a word which is absolutely common in my vocabulary. I don't use it as much as I did but as a boy everybody I knew called each other 'love'. ***Roy Hattersley***

Northerners Don't All Sound the Same

Of course, to southerners, a northern voice is just a northern voice, never mind the subtle differences between a Norwich accent and a North Wales accent, or dare I say a Yorkshire one and a Lancashire one.

❝ *There probably is nothing similar between a Geordie accent and a Scouse accent, they don't share any characteristics at all, yet people would describe them both as a 'northern' accent. And in films or sketch shows, it's always 'Ee by gum'. I don't know anybody in my life who's ever said the words 'Ee by gum'. I don't know anybody who says 'Happen as maybe'. I don't know anybody who uses the word 't'' instead of the word 'the'. I've never been t'pub. I've never been t'park. What does that mean? I don't understand it. And the other thing is, every time a band from the North are interviewed in any music magazine and they'll swear, it's always spelt 'fookin''. 'Fookin.'' Who says that? Could you imagine that: 'Come outside and I'll kick your fooking head in.' Who says 'fooking'?* ***Justin Moorhouse***

❝ *There's one woman in Coronation Street, Mrs Battersby, who has got the most brilliant accent. I think she comes from West Orton on the outskirts of Bolton, between Bolton and Wigan, 'cos her accent is just bang on. But Liz McDonald's accent ... and this is not a criticism ... but it's a Yorkshire accent, a broad Yorkshire accent. I would think that's somewhere like Barnsley, maybe Sheffield, maybe Leeds, maybe Hunslett. And you know, whilst it might be OK for people to think, 'Oh well, it's only northerners, you all speak the same; same vowels, Lancashire and Yorkshire,' there is something of a historical difference between the two places. I think it should have been explained.* ***Stuart Maconie***

Words, Words, Words

There are some northern words and phrases that are so wonderful, so fabulously quirky, that you couldn't make them up.

We had one bloke who was a tractor driver, called Dick Hudson, who worked in our nursery and he used to go out and do the mowing. He'd come in in the morning and sit in the mess room and have his pint of tea, tea the colour of brown leather. And he'd knock that back. We started work at eight o'clock but it'd be half past nine before Dick got out of the mess room onto his tractor. And he'd go out mowing and he'd do enormous circles round the trees on the playing field and then come back for about half past three and sit in his chair again till five. And he would go home every night and say to his wife, 'Eee, take me boots off, lass, I've had a grueller.' Which meant, 'Take my boots off, darling, I've had rather a hard day.' I love that. So I still say to my wife sometimes, 'Eee, lass, take me boots off, I've had a grueller.'
Alan Titchmarsh

'Gradely' – I still use that. 'Gradely' means 'good', you know: 'That was a gradely game of football.' And 'reet' glad. I don't say that as much as I used to do. And I love it when somebody calls me 'chuck', when I meet one of me mum's friends and

they call me 'chuck'. There's something really nice and warm about that. ***Wayne Hemingway***

The whole point about language is that it's changing all the time and English is evolving at a faster rate than ever before because of the Internet and global communications. The word 'whatever', for instance, clearly comes from the Caribbean. People now use it to mean 'bog off and sort it out yourself' or 'just bog off and leave me alone'. Such an innocent-looking little word. Its impact is all in the delivery and the gesture that goes with it. 'Charva' is another of my favourites, although I believe the southerners nicked that one from up north and changed it to 'chav', which is annoying. Both forms refer to someone with more market Burberry than is respectable and larger, heavier earrings than would seem bearable for people with normal earlobes.

There are other regional words that I love and have started to adopt even though they have nothing to do with my roots or where I currently live. I use them simply because I like them … like 'flarch', which is a West Cumbrian word for someone who is a bit of a fraud, a creep or an arse-licker. Or 'doolally', meaning a bit bonkers. My mother would always refer to Mrs Johnson over the road as being a bit 'doolally' when she did something a bit mad and menopausal. Mind you, she did run off with the bank manager and he turned out to be gay and she had to come home again …

In Yorkshire, when their kids are feeling too poorly to go to school their mums will write a letter to Miss saying they're in bad 'feckle', which is much more colourful than saying they have a sore throat. Some words from my childhood have disappeared from my vocabulary altogether, like 'gulley', or a 'ginnel', which, if you're from

Yorkshire, was a funny short cut on the way to school – an alley. If you talked about a gulley today in Camden I imagine they would think you were talking about a pet seagull. And anyway, gulleys would be too dangerous for kids to walk down now, especially in Camden. Another word that has all but disappeared, even in its native northeast, is the word for 'freckles', which is 'furry ticklers'. We should run a campaign to reclaim that one. Some other favourites of mine are 'mardy', meaning 'fed up', and 'mither' meaning to 'worry', both with apparently Midlands or Black Country origins.

'Our baby's crapped his kecks.' You know what that one means? 'Our baby has shit his pants,' basically. Or, 'I'm going down the cut to catch some perch.' Means 'I'm going to the canal to catch a perch' – to go fishing. **Noddy Holder**

Until attitudes change, accent discrimination will have a significant impact on the way we see each other. Or is it class discrimination? Because as we all know, in this country, class is all-important. We can spot class in all its infinite shades of grey up and down the scale in all its scary detail and accent is our microscope.

I'll close with my own all-time-favourite northern phrase – Tin Tin Tin – meaning, what else? *It's not in the tin.*

CHAPTER FIVE

Transport

It comes as no surprise to most people how much of the North there actually is. I live near a town called Haltwhistle in Northumberland, which is officially the centre of Great Britain, not to be confused with the centre of England – that honour goes to Meriden, a nice little place in the West Midlands. But what is really surprising is that most people think Haltwhistle is the North, the proper North. Here we are 20 odd miles west of Newcastle and within rambling distance of Hadrian's Wall … but there is a scary amount of Great Britain still to come north of Haltwhistle. I suppose it's all relative, and as if to prove that the people of Haltwhistle feel like they are in the middle rather than in the far north, they have built the second-largest open-air pool in the North – a wondrous heated open-air experience that effectively throws the V-sign up at southerners who stop there and think the place is so north it might as well be at the North Pole. They stand next to the brown sign saying 'Outdoor Pool' and point to it ostentatiously and wait for southerners to pass and look gobsmacked and frankly amazed.

When you live somewhere like Haltwhistle, you know that the place is only just tickling the edge of the north of the country. But tell this to a southerner and they are usually astonished, because anything further north than, say, York is the far north and when they find out that there's a whole lot more north further up than York they are truly shocked, because they have no trouble picturing us all living in igloos and fishing for seals through holes in the ice. The point I wish to make here is that just because we live in the North, miles from London, this is no excuse for ignoring the fact that we need to get about the place and depriving us of a cheap and efficient transport network.

Transport, like everything else in the UK, is entirely southeast-centric. If there's a decent train service out of Paddington, or a convenient flight out of Heathrow, then as far as Whitehall is concerned it's sorted. Because surely, apart from the odd trip to head office and the annual holiday to Blackpool or Benidorm, what would the rest of us need with a decent transport system anyway?

There's something else very unfortunate about people from the North: they are allowed to travel. They don't stay where they should, so you find them all over the place. You find them on beaches and, wonderful though they are, they come up and talk to you. Well, I don't mind being talked to for a second, but people from the North will tell you their entire life story, their relatives, their work situation, where they went on holiday the year before, bless them, they really think they are interesting. This is a terrible problem with people in the North – they are lovely people but they are not interesting. ***Michael Winner***

Let the Train Take the Strain

Here's a novel idea: let's concentrate on getting rail transport right *between* places in the North and the honorary north rather than just to and from London. Access to the capital is invariably the Government's priority, whether it's from Brighton or from York and true, we're pleased that these routes have improved. I know we all complain about it, and no doubt if you live in the far northwest or in mid-Wales, it's still a nightmare to get to and from the capital. I can remember, although only just, the time when you used to have to get a sleeper from Berwick-on-Tweed to London to make it worthwhile going there for a day or two, never mind just for the day like you can now. And I have to admit that, bad as GNER can be at times, on a good day they can now get you from Newcastle to King's Cross (274 miles) in an astonishing 2 hours 50 minutes. And they will let you buy a nice cheese-and-ham toastie or, if you're feeling flush, some *seriously* decent food in the dining car.

But what if I want to get to Manchester from Newcastle (134 miles)? I get the Trans-Pennine 'Express' (so called). The journey's only half as far as London but, if the service runs to schedule, it will take only 12 minutes less. What's more the train will have just three carriages, each full to bursting. People will be trying to work on their laptops or failing to keep their small children quiet. And there's an overwhelming smell of loo freshener (almost worse than the pong of the loo itself, in my view). If you're lucky, you might get an instant coffee, though these conditions will apply:

- If the person they employ to push the trolley has shown up for work that morning
- If the trolley they have given this person is fully operational, as in it has enough hot water
- If this trolley and the person they have employed to pour hot water on to a Styrofoam cup of coffee granules can manage to get through to you past all the enormous cases and bags that are blocking the aisles.

What do you mean 6 hours? I want Newcastle, man, not New York!

Hasn't anyone ever stopped to consider that there might be lot of people up north who need to get from Liverpool to Carlisle, or Stockport to Leeds, or Middlesbrough to Manchester? Don't they know that people get fed up with having to stand for the whole journey when they have bought a full-price ticket? That they might want something decent to eat and drink? Obviously not.

“ *I travel twice a week on Midland Mainline. It's getting better but there was a time a couple of years ago when, if the train arrived on time or within ten minutes of time, the passengers applauded.* **Roy Hattersley**

Getting from one big northern city to another is hard enough, but try getting from Sheffield to Ipswich or from Middlesbrough to Torquay. Or Newcastle to Cardiff, just 298 miles but it takes an astonishing six hours by rail, (assuming you make all the connections on time) *and* it would cost far more than a no-frills flight to Europe (£162 return). Even easyJet haven't bothered with this one. Far too fiddly, though they can offer you a cheaper, quicker trip from Luton to Athens in one hop, no trouble at all.

“ *We've got a funny-shaped country. You look at France or Spain or Germany and they're not quite round but they're kind of compact. We've got this stretched-out country with dog-legs and things. So if you need to get to a place like Morecambe Bay or Whitehaven you've got to get round the dog-leg. On paper it looks like a simple journey but you might as well double the time you think it's going to take. And that's a real issue. Some of the journeys in England are harder to make than flying from Perth to Sydney in Australia.* **Wayne Hemingway**

Luton Airport

The same is true for us northerners when we want to go abroad. Nine times out of ten we have to get to one of the London airports before we can fly anywhere. Or else we face a three-hour drive to Manchester or four hours to Birmingham and that will probably add another £200 to our holiday in Florida or Spain, because regional airports are often more expensive than Gatwick, or Heathrow or even Luton. And even then you'll be lucky to get a direct flight. All because we live up north and not within striking distance of Gatwick or Heathrow.

What's so ridiculous about where I live is that every time I fly to the States I have to spend four or five hours (and an obscene amount of money to boot) getting to an airport down south. I get on the plane and then what happens? I find myself travelling northwards because the flight from London to New York is normally routed over Scotland. So on a clear day, some eight hours or so after leaving home, I can look down and see my house again.

On the Buses

Public transport is truly a way of life up north. People meet at the bus stop, chat at the bus stop – shock, horror, yes they really do – and go to the shops on the bus. I can think of no nicer way to get around than sitting on the top deck of the bus having a good old nose into other people's front gardens or even straight into their front bedrooms. When I was a kid growing up in leafy Solihull in the West Midlands there was one particular house on the bus route where you could see right into a woman's bedroom – it became quite a daily attraction. I am sure she knew exactly what she was doing but imagine: a busload of adolescent boys and girls … Once you get the hang of buses they are infinitely more convenient than cars in town, and infinitely preferable to going down onto the Central Line and faffing about changing lines. And coach travel too, when you are going inter-city (as we used to say), is such a marvellous northern institution, still incredibly cheap and you sit next to the same person for so long you become bosom pals, possibly marry and certainly exchange Christmas cards.

London Transport Hell

One of the big pluses of living in the North or the honorary north is obviously the relative lack of traffic and the relative ease with which we get about in our cities. Which brings us on to London traffic. If cabs were free I might consider living in London, at least during the week, because anything that avoids the whole process of having to park – ever again – gets my vote. But unless you have a few hundred pounds a week to spare or your own chauffeur you can forget it. Have you been in a London cab recently? Unbelievably expensive. For what seems like about two years now if you arrive at King's Cross, like I do from the North, the taxis have been made to do a huge detour because they are building some massive new train interchange to France. Which will indeed be nice because presumably we won't have to get out at King's Cross and then get all our holiday luggage down the steps to the Tube. Steps, did you notice I said steps? No one has worked out that there are thousands and thousands of people like you and me who arrive at King's Cross with a lot of luggage. Hello, well of course we arrive with luggage. It's taken us hours to get to London so most of us are staying at least one night. No escalator and no slopy things for cases with wheels even. No, just steps. Nice. So we all have to get our luggage down the steps. And break our backs and trip other people up in the process. Last time I asked someone to help me down with my case – obviously I spent a minute or two selecting someone since there might be serial muggers, drug addicts, etc., or someone who might just go and stab me for the hell of it because I held them up for a few seconds. I chose well because he was very nice indeed and helped me down, but when he handed my case back he said, 'I wouldn't do that here love, not again. I'm an undercover policeman and we're tracking people who run off with people's bags when they do exactly this.' So now I have to lug everything down the steps like everyone else. At least in the northeast we have a nice efficient Metro service, which is well organized with lifts and escalators and is completely buggie- and wheelchair-friendly – try using the London Underground in a wheelchair. No chance.

So anyway, often I have no choice but to take a cab to get to the hotel, and because of this new interchange thing the cab drivers have to go about three blocks north first before they can go south again and head for town, which costs about £3.50 before you even get started. Then, after that, it all gets horribly cumulative – once you've clocked up the first £5 the dial starts to go bananas and the numbers flick round so fast they're a blur and before you know it you've clocked up a shocking and appalling £20 to go two miles.

All the cab drivers that pick you up from King's Cross ask where you've come from, and once you say Durham or Darlington or Glasgow they go all patronizing and stupid, telling you that they have a second cousin who lives in Middlesbrough – 'Do you know them? I went up to see them once for a holiday and came back early because the weather was so perishing. Do you like it up there? Oh, right, well, it takes all sorts ... And what time did you leave this morning? Six o'clock? No! Never! Was it dark?' Of course, by now it's 11am and everyone's in their short sleeves as it's summer. You left at six in the morning and put your thermals on and a big coat, which you now have to lug around all day. People in London always milk this like mad. You arrive at the meeting and they all say, 'Gosh, have you come all the way from Newcastle this morning?' Like you lived in the Third World. 'Really? It must have been really cold.' And you feel really stupid with the wrong clothes on entirely, holding your coat and your jumpers and feeling like someone who showed up at a fancy-dress party with the wrong outfit on. They like making you feel like that. Makes them feel a bit better about having to live an hour and a half away from proper fresh air, and having to pay half a day's salary for a drink in the pub with their mates.

London can also be really scary if you're not used to it, and the Tube is the scariest thing of all. If you've been brought up in Barnsley or Burnham-on-Sea and you get plonked in London for a job interview or a first day at college, you are completely at sea. The place is a nightmare if you're a newcomer or stranger. And people who live in London totally underestimate what a confusing and intimidating place it can be. People from the North who move down to London, and sadly so many of us need to at one time or another, find the whole thing completely daunting. Why on earth wouldn't we? Most of us have only been there on a school trip to the Natural History Museum, or once or twice to Oxford Street to see the lights, and then wham, we are off to London trying to figure out the Tube map and the *A–Z*, and where the hell are we going to live, and who do we share with. Answering an ad in the *Evening Standard* for a flat share is so risky you might well chum up with some people coming out of Wandsworth prison. Everything is frightening, and how are you going to find your way around?

The Tube's a fantastic idea. You want to go from there to there, oh you've to go via Embankment. Then swap to the Circle Line, go north on the Victoria for two stops – come back, you've not got the right travel card – and when you get there ... I've done this myself – I've changed tubes three times and got somewhere and they've said, 'Why didn't you just walk? It's 150 yards.'
Justin Moorhouse

The thing that would drive me most mad about living in London is getting anywhere. Londoners always boast about how easy it is to get from their house into the West End – 'Takes me 30 minutes,' they say. Yes, 30 minutes at 3am on Christmas Day, but not when you *want* to get there, more like 90 minutes of stopping and starting, using up masses of petrol, and £5 for the congestion charge – that's more like it.

Driving in London is officially pants. Londoners pay £150 million a year to drive in their own city with the congestion charge. London has the most vehicle crime of any region in England – a fifth of the country's total. Over 55,000 cars were stolen in London last year, more than three times as many as in the southwest and over four times the number stolen in the northeast.

Londoners spend so much time in their cars. People who live in London and the southeast spend on average

86 minutes a day getting to and from work, which, with a bit added on for trips to the video shop or to pick up a pizza and so on, might be something like two hours a day in traffic. Two hours a day! And that's five days a week, plus an hour a day at weekends getting to and from Sainsbury's and the squash court or the dry-cleaners. That's 12 hours a week, 48 hours a month, an appalling 21 days a year. Just sitting in traffic listening to some stupid Radio1 DJ or Steve Wright's Sunday love songs. Get the picture? Sitting in traffic for our friends in the South is a way of life.

❝ *I went to London once for an audition and they flew me down and they flew me back. I spent more time in the taxi from the airport to the audition and back again than I did flying to and from Manchester. It was only about five miles and everybody accepts this! I'd be going mad, I'd be like Michael Douglas in* Falling Down. *I'd be getting out of my car and going on the rampage. They just sit there going, 'This is what it's like.'*
Justin Moorhouse

Has the congestion charge made any difference? Well apparently it has, the latest boast being that it has reduced congestion by 17 per cent. Which is a step in the right direction that's for sure. Doesn't mean we have to like it though …

❝ *Then the congestion charge. I thought you passed a barrier where you'd pay. What worries me about the congestion charge isn't the £5 – I don't mind that, you can have that … It's this awful fear that if you don't pay, draconian penalties, £80 a day or something, kick in. I mean it is awful victimization. I'm a motorist talking from the heart here.* ***William Roache***

Driving Us Crazy

Because people spend so long in their cars in the South, driving there is beyond horrible. People spend so long in traffic that they end up having to do everything in their cars – reading their post, doing a morning's work on the phone, putting their make-up on, having a shave, sitting their exams, everything. As if there were any further need to prove that our quality of life is infinitely better up here

than it is down there! No wonder southern drivers are so aggressive and will cut you up as soon as look you. They invented road rage down there, you know, because getting in and out of the right lane is a matter of life or death to them. You don't mess with London drivers.

“ *I remember the first time I drove in London. I was absolutely terrified, and I was astonished at how vigorous they were with their driving, how ugly they could be. And there's this feeling, particularly with London drivers, that they never make mistakes.* ***Alan Titchmarsh***

Drivers in the South are the meanest, most selfish people. They won't give you an inch, they'll never let you into a queue and they cut you up all the time. No wonder London is covered with spiteful, horrid speed bumps and they need speed cameras on every lamppost. Serves them right.

“ *If you wait at the side of a road in Manchester, it might not be the first person who lets you out, it might not be the second, but generally I would say it's the third or the fourth. But once you start to drive in London you wait for the first, second, third, fourth, fifth, sixth, seventh, eighth, ninth car and then you realize: 'Right, OK, so what I'm going to have to do is just push my way out.'* ***Mark Radcliffe***

In the North people are relatively courteous, they wait their turn and let you go in front of them. And most northern drivers would probably stop and help you out if you have a puncture. But not in the South. You could be stranded for a fortnight on a side road, especially if you're driving a Porsche or something. That really gets up people's noses. You'd better look out if you've got a posh car because car envy is akin to penis envy and it all adds inevitably to the road rage. The sad thing is, once you've had the experience of driving down south it tends to corrupt you and before you know it you're ducking and diving just like a London cabbie.

> *When I'm in a traffic jam I'm always looking for a way to nip out of it. You do that when you're driving in London. But they don't like that in the North, there is an etiquette, so if there is a queue of people, they don't want some smart-arse jumping out from the side and getting ahead. They will all queue very dutifully, very politely and they don't like it if some southerner tries to get ahead of the game. They go mad.* **Carole Malone**

Baby, You Can Drive My Car

Car ownership is lower in the North than in the South. For instance in the northeast it is lower than anywhere else in the UK, but it is catching up fast and we need to ensure that our northern transport systems get the funding they deserve otherwise we are in danger of having the same problems as they have down south. An astonishing 6.3 per cent of households in the southeast region own three cars and 2.1 per cent own four or more – no wonder no one can find anywhere to park.

But it's only going to get worse and if we don't do something about it we're going to end up with the same level of congestion up here as they have down south. All of our major cities are getting clogged up and soon the whole bloody country will come to one bad-tempered gridlock and no one will be able to drive anywhere.

It's a well-known fact that the more roads you build the quicker they fill up with traffic – the M25 tells us that every day – but that doesn't seem to stop us. By the way, at 118 miles, the M25 is the longest ring road in the world, although it's not a complete circle, which means that there must be a lot of people doing three-point turns at the end of it, I guess, or getting stuck in a jam when it narrows down to two lanes. Maybe that's what's causing the hold-ups.

Traffic Update

As usual, when it comes to traffic and traffic reports London thinks it has the monopoly. I accept that they have vastly more traffic there than we do in the North but when we're listening to a national radio station we would like the reports to reflect where we live, too. Please. Which doesn't seem unreasonable. To me.

“ *If they're doing a traffic report on national radio or TV, it's about the traffic in Oxford Street or the Mall or somewhere like that. We don't give a toss up here what the traffic's like in Oxford Street or down the Mall or if it's pissing down with rain down the Strand. Tell us what the national traffic's like; tell us if there's a massive hold-up on the M6 or on the M1 so we're not sitting in it for hours. It's all based on me, me, me, me, London, London, London down there.* ***Noddy Holder***

So stop giving us all the traffic news from the Hammersmith flyover all the time when we live in Oban or Truro. OK? It couldn't be more meaningless. Look, haven't they got local radio like we have? They can fiddle around with the dials and find their own traffic news like we have to, thank you very much.

You hear traffic reports, and I've never been, but there's no way I'd ever want to go to the Hanger Lane Gyratory. It just sounds like a terrible place to be and it's always closed. And the North Circular, that's ... but it's down south, it doesn't work, does it? ***Justin Moorhouse***

The Hanger Lane Gyratory System (see below) a horrid place? Surely not.

Parking Mad

In the South it's not that easy to get out of your car because you can never find anywhere to leave the wretched thing. You drive round and round like the Flying Dutchman, doomed to spending the next seven years in a sea of traffic unless there's a miracle and you find a space big enough to squeeze into. And to do that you need money. Londoners pay hundreds of pounds for parking permits (and yet there are 13,000 more parking permits than parking spaces in Kensington and Chelsea alone) and are penalized with a whopping £300 million a year in fines and congestion charges. There is a lot of money in parking. The city of Westminster alone reportedly gets £65 million a year in parking revenue. Mostly from John Prescott. Parking spaces are at such a premium that some people never actually move their cars for fear of losing a precious slot. I used to live in Chiswick and if ever you actually managed to find a space outside your house, or within walking distance of it, you were so chuffed that you never wanted to move your car – ever. So you left it there for weeks and took the Tube or the bus to Sainsbury's. You soon discovered two major drawbacks to this strategy: you could never manage to carry as much shopping home as you used to get in the boot of the car and if you didn't turn over the engine for a fortnight, the battery would go flat. It was a bit self-defeating really.

Whereas in the North … it's a breeze. You actually do have a choice. If you don't fancy walking, you can drive to work. They won't charge you to park there. Then you can drive home for lunch, popping into the corner shop, or the post office or the chippy on the way. You can park the car right outside your own front door. You won't have to go round the block five times in the vain hope that your

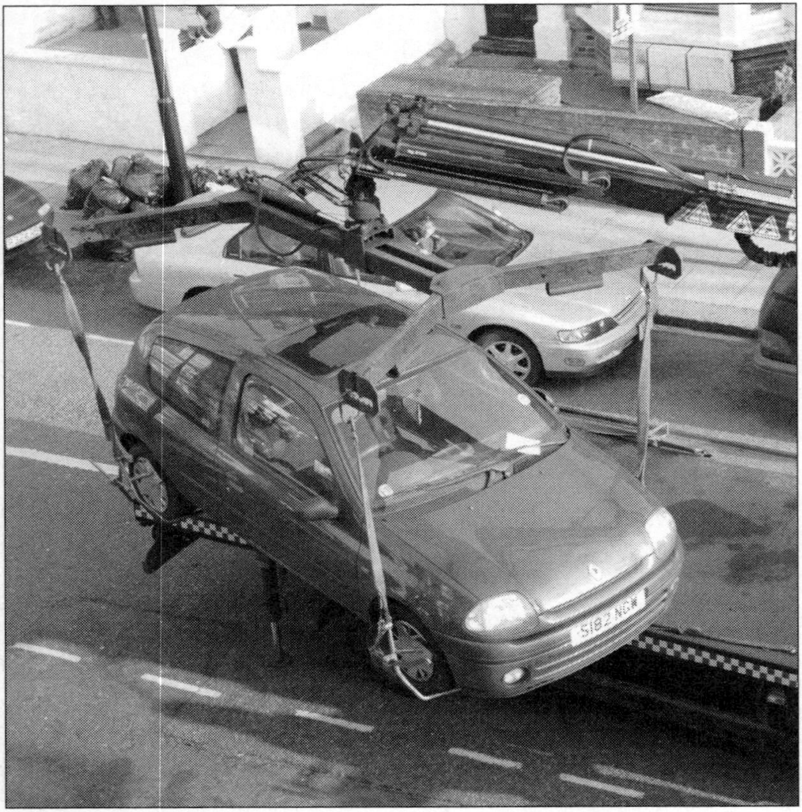

When did you last find a parking place in London? 1985? Mmm, thought so.

neighbours will be foolish enough to drive off somewhere, thus leaving you with a nanosecond window of opportunity to nab their space. Well, OK, so it's not always this easy, but by comparison it's a doddle.

Car-parking etiquette is so different in the North. We point out the spare spaces to one another and sometimes, if we leave before the ticket's run out of time, we will pass it on to the next person. (Though if it's someone you don't like, you make sure the ticket you give them has only got about two minutes left to run and then you can have a good laugh when you see the look on their face and they're forced to go and pay.)

Walk the Walk

When you're a pedestrian in the South you need ideally to wear a white pollution mask to protect you from the exhaust fumes, like they do in Tokyo, but you do feel a bit of a prat. No need for that in the North, of course, but having been a pedestrian with a foot in both camps so to speak I have to concede that they're less likely to run you over on the road down there. If I were a cynic I would say this is because the traffic is forced to a snail's pace most of the time so the drivers never get up enough speed to do any lasting damage and they hardly ever have their reflexes put to the test. Traffic flow in the North is that much faster, so you have to take a bit more care when crossing the road.

> *When I moved to London I was quite surprised that no matter where you were walking, people stopped for you to cross a zebra crossing. They don't in the North, you've got to basically make a run for it.* ***Mark Radcliffe***

You do have to watch out at the traffic lights in London, though. Don't expect any driver to hesitate in your favour when the lights go green. I thought I was safe when I tried to cross a bit of the Great Western Road in Hammersmith the other day, only the lights changed before I got to the other side. I survived – just – but if I had misjudged it by one more millisecond you would have had to scrape me off the tarmac. Some of those drivers had been sitting there deliberately revving up. Maybe they wanted something to break the boredom or relieve the frustration that builds up after an average Tuesday at work and figured that running a pedestrian down would do the trick.

No, give me some nice dozy northern drivers any day of the week, never mind on an average Tuesday. You know, the old boys with porkpie hats, sat low in their seats, peering over the steering wheels like Kilroy. They might dither about and hold you up for a few moments but they're never going to be aggressive with it.

It's a Small World

Sometimes the country seems enormous, and sometimes it feels titchy. No one expects a journey that involves travelling by both land and sea to be record-breakingly fast. Part of the point of going to out-of-the-way places is to enjoy the trip itself, isn't it? It's clearly going to be difficult, though if you think remote automatically equals deserted then you should treat the following as a cautionary tale.

A couple of years back I decided to go to Knoydart in northwest Scotland. Apparently, it's the remotest place in Great Britain – so isolated that it is only reachable by boat. A boat that only runs twice a week. If the weather is fair. Off I went, looking forward to solitude and peace and quiet, only to discover that I was not alone in my quest. Before you get to the boat leg of the journey you have to take a train that weaves its way through some of the most stunning scenery in the Scottish Highlands. So, who do you think my fellow travellers were, in the three small carriages that make up this train, on its way to connect with the twice-weekly boat that will take you to the remotest part of the country? I met Mel and Sue off the telly, Chris Smith (then in the Cabinet) and his entourage, and someone I was at college with and hadn't seen in 20 years. Small world, but I wouldn't want to have to paint it, as the saying goes.

CHAPTER SIX

Culture

At last we have a bit more money in our pockets up north and, on the whole, life is better than it's ever been. But there's still one major area that needs sorting out: when it comes to culture and arts, the North–South divide is alive and thriving. Oh yes, London and the southeast are holding on to most of our national treasures and will they give any of them up? What do you think?

A National Scandal

For a start, what's with this *national* business? The National Gallery, the National Film Theatre, the National Maritime Museum, the National Theatre (and the British Museum): where are they? Oh, in London, within easy reach of our friends in the South. But what about the rest of us, the

majority of the population, the ones who don't live in London?

Come the revolution we can begin to put things right, and my proposal is that we should make a start by shifting some of the nation's buildings and art treasures away from the overcrowded south and put them in the North. For example, why not put Buckingham Palace in a place where people can't avoid seeing it … like the central reservation of the M6 or the top of Spaghetti Junction? And open the whole building to the public while we're at it? Someone would have to stop the corgis from being squished by a juggernaut but the Queen's surely got enough staff for that. And then once Buck House has moved north, we can get the royal family to make Windsor Castle its permanent home. Admittedly, this accommodation might prove to be a bit pokey, and it does lie under a major flight path, but we all have to make sacrifices in life, don't we?

I suppose people in the South have got to make themselves feel a bit better about living within reach of the South Circular, and so they make out that it is so much more happening, so much more cultured where they live. But the way they talk, you'd think we never went to art galleries up north. Well, of course we would go if there were more of them, and if they weren't all sitting within a square mile of one another, you know where …

The British media invariably portray London as the home of all things desirable, the magnet for talent and resources, the sole arbiter of value and success. This doesn't happen in other European countries. Most of them promote their major cities as cultural centres in their own right, they don't ghettoize them like we do.

When you think of Spain and the great cities you don't just think of Madrid. There's Barcelona as well, which is on an equal footing, and in Italy you've got Rome, you've got Milan and Florence, and all these places have got their own cultural identities, and I think the one thing they could probably do is spread out some of the collections and let other people see them. Because not everybody can go to London and see a painting. You can't take a bus of school kids to London just to see something by da Vinci ... put it on a bus, get it in Huddersfield. ***Justin Moorhouse***

Better still, why not mount a series of travelling exhibitions, and I do mean 'travelling'. Get all of that art out of those stuffy southern galleries and trundle them onto the trains, especially the cross-country cattle trucks we have to put up with in the North, because we could certainly do with some on-rail entertainment when we are trying to get about on public transport. They could put a different Renaissance masterpiece on the tea trolley every week and wheel it up and down the aisles to cheer us all up. You'd have to leave some realistic copies behind in London for the American tourists to gawp at, but they'll not know the difference.

Paintings that are saved for the nation, the great collections and everything ... I mean, I have no problem with them being in London some of the time but it's not difficult to move a painting, is it? Why should a painting be permanently anywhere? You know, we are all part of the country, we all pay tax towards the country, so we all have a stake and an ownership in the great artefacts of the age. Why shouldn't exhibitions travel a bit more? ***Mark Radcliffe***

You'd expect the capital city to dominate to an extent, but London is just plain thuggish about how much of the nation's resources and wealth it hangs on to. The following *national* institutions are all based in London:

Football – Wembley
Rugby – Twickenham
Tennis – Wimbledon
Cricket – Lords
The National Theatre
The National Film Theatre
English National Opera
English National Ballet
The Royal Opera House
The Royal Philharmonic Orchestra
The National Maritime Museum
The British Museum

No wonder tourists hardly ever go anywhere but London when nearly everything labelled 'National' is there. Come on, you visitors, head for the North for the newest and trendiest on the British culture scene.

Art for Whose Sake?

Let's talk about art for a start. London has so much more than its fair share: 16 out of our 22 major art galleries are there. All those priceless masterpieces owned by the nation, are … guess where? … slap bang in the middle of London. They've even got the *Blue Peter* garden. Which is fine and dandy for the people who live there (and all the Japanese tourists who keep our economy buoyant) but infuriatingly not handy for the rest of us. To add insult to injury, they talk about the North like it's a culture-free zone, like we still think spam is tinned meat, like bingo with chips and gravy is as clever as culture gets up north, and if we want some action we go to the Co-op and watch them use the bacon slicer.

Southerners think we all live in drab streets in dreary houses with nasty reproduction prints and a trio of Hilda Ogden-type flying ducks on our woodchip-papered walls – but not in a post-postmodern ironic sense like they do in Holland Park. They think our sense of style is brash, vulgar and in your face and we will never ever get it right because by the time the latest trend has reached the North it's *so* last season, you know, so *provincial*. Have you noticed how people in the South pronounce the words *provincial* and the *provinces* with a bit of a sneer in their voices or if not that, then with a touch of false pity? The cheek of it. Like we haven't seen their bling outfits and dodgy nail extension bars, and Young Tories and nasty horrid ruchy curtains. And it was them that invented Brentford Nylons, not us.

“ *They don't think we actually go to galleries, or go to museums. Basically, they think we're thick and that we have no interest in it, but we probably have far more interest than they do down there.* ***Noddy Holder***

So … it has fallen to me to put the record straight. How much interest is there in culture up north? How often do we go to the theatre, exhibitions and museums? Is it true that we're not that fussed about culture with a capital C and art with a capital A? Maybe, horror of horrors, Philip Wakem in *The Mill on the Floss* is right about what he calls 'the dead level of provincial existence'.

“ *Well, it was suggested that the people in the North want to take the culture and the art from London and spread it their way. This, of course, is absolute nonsense; if they wanted it they would have it. If there was a demand for it, it would be there because they would have raised charities or raised events or lobbied their local councillors. They don't want culture in the North ... I've never liked cultured people, you know, they think they are very clever.* ***Michael Winner***

Well, what about the Baltic Centre for Contemporary Art in Gateshead, for example? It has been hugely successful, so much so that it attracted a million visitors in its first year. It was part of the £500 million spent on regenerating Tyneside that includes the Sage (see below), which opened for business in December 2004, just around the corner.

From the moment they launched what is said to be the biggest and most ambitious £12 million cultural programme, events at this fantastically eye-catching concert hall have been booked up months in advance. And look at the Royal Ballet in Birmingham: ever since it relocated from London in 1990 their audiences have been getting more and more enthusiastic – they regularly achieve 98% sell-outs. And then there's the Tate St Ives, which attracted 237,000 visitors in 2004. So I think we can safely say that there is indeed an appetite in the North for culture, Mr Winner. And how.

Take that great northern landmark in the sky, Antony Gormley's amazing *Angel of the North*, for instance (see below). This has two claims to fame: firstly, it's the biggest sculpture in Britain – 20 metres high with 54-metre wide wings – and secondly, it is one of the most viewed pieces of art, not just in the country but in the world. They reckon that it's seen by more than 90,000 people a day: that's at least one person per second. See ... you're impressed ... though perhaps you should know that because it's sited virtually on the central reservation of the A1 a lot of those people are coincidentally driving past in their cars or sitting on the train on the East Coast London–Edinburgh line, so they haven't exactly planned their visit. But the

wonderful thing about it is that it is so damned big that, love it or hate it, you can't ignore it. And that's incredible.

Clearly, here in the North and in the honorary north we all like to visit art galleries, we like to go to the theatre, we like to dance, we like to hear world-class music, and we like the opera and the ballet a great deal more than we are given credit for by people in London. We need more of it, much more, but first let's look at what we have got, how much there is in the North already.

Here are a few showy-offy facts about culture and art in the North:

Liverpool is in the *Guinness Book of Records* as the capital of pop music, because it has produced more artists who have had a number one hit than any other city in the UK.

Gateshead has one of the most acoustically perfect concert halls in the world: the Sage.

Newcastle has the biggest original art store in the country, all 35,000 square metres of it. It's called the Biscuit Factory and it's great fun … but they don't sell biscuits.

Liverpool has more museums, theatres and galleries than any other city outside London.

Manchester's Imperial War Museum North is breaking all box-office records.

Edinburgh's annual Fringe Festival is the largest comedy event in the world.

Liverpool has the largest collection of Grade II listed buildings outside London.

Leicester's Festival of Light is the largest Divali event in the UK.

Buxton's Festival has become the Glyndebourne of the North – 32,000 tickets were sold in 2004 and the festival has doubled in size in the last four years.

People in the North spend more on buying art than any other region in the UK.

Look how many times Liverpool crops up in that list – that should be noted by all those snotty-nosed people who pulled a face when it succeeded in its bid to be the European City of Culture for 2008. They had a good laugh about that, didn't they? Saying it was a contradiction in terms, which was a sick joke. They just wouldn't let it lie.

“ *It's just because Liverpool has a reputation for being somewhere that had crime problems. And so it was just a knee-jerk reaction, I think, to what was depicted as a very deprived city.* ***Kate Robbins***

OK, the truth is that Liverpool reached an all-time low in 1981, with the Toxteth riots and a grim unemployment rate of 25%, but the place has been transformed in recent years. Tourism is now a huge business – the Beatles tour attracts 600,000 people from all over the world (many of them Japanese since Japan has the largest Beatles fan club in the world), who come to see the famous Penny Lane and the homes of John Lennon and Paul McCartney, as well as the church hall where John and Paul first made music together. It's a fabulous and moving tour and one that even a moderately enthusiastic Beatles fan would enjoy. The Liverpool Tate is an exciting building to visit, full of eye-catching modern art, and the Walker is being expanded beyond recognition. The riverside is unrecognizable and these days you can buy Vivienne Westwood and lattes within spitting distance of the Cavern Club. Liverpool is simply a fantastic place to be in the twenty-first century.

Don't knock it – Liverpool is just fantastic, even more so now than in the 1960s when the Beatles put it bang in the middle of the world stage.

Even Birmingham gets some praise for once, in terms of the arts and culture available there.

> *It's got Stratford and the Royal Shakespeare Company. It's got Symphony Hall and the CBSO, one of the best orchestras in the land. It's got Birmingham Royal Ballet and an art gallery with the finest collection of pre-Raphaelite paintings outside Andrew Lloyd Webber's study. Astonishing things there, all in Birmingham. And I'd go out in my lunch hour thinking, 'Well, I won't find much here, will I, apart from Boots the Chemist.' And it was astonishing. And for ten years I was completely occupied almost every afternoon with something either artistic or cultural, an astonishing output there, which people just don't know about. If you get out there it's there. I think they just keep it quiet.*
> ***Alan Titchmarsh***

Capital Idea

If you don't work in London or never have done, then it seems that no one will take you seriously. For some strange reason the general consensus is that anything that goes on in London is by definition more significant than anything that happens anywhere else. I can only assume that this is part of the smokescreen that people who live in London create in order to make themselves appear more important and sophisticated than the rest of us. 'Oh, I wouldn't live anywhere else,' they say. 'I could spend all day going to galleries and museums and the opera.' Yes, I say to myself, but when did you last actually go to the opera? More to the point, when were you last able to *afford* to go to it?

In my experience, Londoners never bother going to the opera or the theatre, even though it's right there on their doorstep. It's the Japanese and American tourists, and the coach trips from Weston-super-Mare who have queued up in Leicester Square for their theatre tickets who keep these things going and anyway, let's be honest, most of what is on in the West End is a bit crap, isn't it? All those meaningless musicals with no plot visible to the naked eye … I mean, did you see *Starlight Express*? (If you did, by the way, can you just paraphrase the plot for me? A couple of lines will do, nothing fancy, just so that I get the gist.) I see they are thrusting the show onto us in the provinces now, with a country-wide regional tour. Then they'll probably do it on ice and charge us all double.

I have arguments with loads of my mates, who have moved from the Midlands and the North and relocated in London, and they absolutely refuse to move back. They say they'll never move back for any reason whatsoever. And I say, 'Well, what keeps you there?' And what they'll say to me is, 'Well, it's cosmopolitan.' Oh, so Birmingham and Manchester and Liverpool's not cosmopolitan. What are you talking about? 'Oh, we've got museums.' We've got museums up here as well. 'Well, we've got great restaurants.' Oh, we've got great restaurants up here. And then you say to them, 'Well, when was the last time you went to the museum?' 'Well, I've never been to one, but we've got them if I want to.' **Noddy Holder**

It's not that I blame the unfortunate people who live in and around London for not going to see more theatre or doing a weekly trip to the Tate. If I lived in a penthouse overlooking Chelsea Bridge, with more money and free time than sense, then I might be able to stroll into a gallery for a bit of fantastic culture, but for everyone else, by the time they've got back from work to their flat in Muswell Hill or Penge, most of them don't have the energy or indeed the spare cash to pay for a meal let alone a seat at the Royal Opera.

❝ *The only time I ever go to a gallery or a show or a museum is when one of my friends from the North comes and they have never been to the Science Museum and that's the only time I go because during the week I'm too tired. And at the weekend I can't be bothered to sit in two and a half hours of traffic to get to one of those museums. Once you get there it's fine but you know, it's too much like hard work.* **Carole Malone**

And can you believe how much it costs to go to the theatre in London? It's not uncommon to pay £50 a ticket, and the opera … well, £50 will buy you a seat with a restricted view of the stage, so if you want something decent you'll probably have to shell out more like £100 for your evening's entertainment. I imagine watching *La Bohème* at Covent Garden would be an exquisite experience, but it's only a nineteenth-century soap opera with music, isn't it? And it's in a funny foreign language. No wonder most Londoners prefer to watch *EastEnders* at home before popping out for a quick one and a quiz at their local boozer. Twice the fun at a fraction of the price.

❝ *What London offers is a kind of life that is in some sense continental; there are galleries here, there are music places, there is always a concert, there is nearly always an opera, there is nearly always a play that you want to see. It is where things happen. And that is why we stay, it's for what it offers us.* **Brian Sewell**

The sad truth is that the North has a great deal less spent on it on the arts than London and the South, and the figures are nothing less than scandalous. London was the biggest recipient of Arts Council grant-in-aid subsidy in 2000, nobbling 48.3% of the total distributed to all ten regions in the country, and although things are improving, the imbalance is still marked.

You actually can't beat London for culture, you really can't; it is the centre of the universe culturally. It's just we're all so exhausted, we're just such dried old husks at the end of the day. But despite the fact that most of them never make use of the culture and art on their doorsteps, boy do they go on about the cultured South. Southerners really, really show off about culture. 'Oh, we so love the opera and the theatre and the exhibitions, it's all so awfully, awfully stimulating,' they guffaw. Yes, right. When was the last time they went to the opera, then? And when they say theatre, Snow White *at Wimbledon panto doesn't count. And the Swinging Blue Jeans with only one original member doesn't count, either.* ***Jenny Eclair***

Unfortunately, much of the money spent on trouble-shooting the problem of badly distributed culture has been directed at the people who apparently need it most but who have entirely different priorities. These days there is so much arts money being thrown at sink estates up north that schoolkids in Middlesbrough can only sigh with disbelief at the thought of the Royal Shakespeare Company doing their umpteenth workshop with them and they wilt at the prospect of yet another Arts Council-funded project with the Royal Ballet. Most of them would prefer the money spent on getting them a decent breakfast or some new trainers, but I suppose someone has to keep writing blockbusting movies and musicals like *Billy Elliot*.

For the most part the North doesn't get its fair share of support for the arts and when it does manage to catch some crumbs from London's overladen cultural dinner table, a lot of it is simply ill-conceived ... like Tracey Emin reportedly getting £60,000 for the sculpture or installation or whatever it is that now stands in front of the Oratory in Liverpool. This work of art (conceived, by the way, by a southern artist for the enlightenment of the North) comes in the form of a tiny bird (is it a robin, or a swift, or some sort of 'everybird'? – nobody knows, including the artist herself) on a 4-metre high bronze pole. Tracey Emin calls the work *Roman Standard* and says that it stands for strength and femininity, while the bird, being an 'angel of the earth' represents freedom, as well as being a tribute to the city's legendary Liver Bird. At the unveiling in February 2005 I'm told she informed everyone that she had decided to accept the commission because she had such fun memories of the city. And do you know why? Because she'd had her best ever orgasm there. She's just having a laugh, isn't she? Sixty thousand quid for a bird on a stick and an innuendo? Though I suppose you could now legitimately ask her, 'Do you come here often?' (Sorry, couldn't resist it.)

What seems glaringly obvious to me is that rather than spend so much lottery money on new projects up north, the easiest and cleverest thing to do would be to redistribute what is already down in London. Some people would get a seat in the House of Lords for suggesting that.

Brian Sewell fuelled the debate somewhat in 2003 when he said that an exhibition by postwar artists should not be put on at the Baltic in Gateshead because London was the centre of the art world. He claimed that people in the capital are more sophisticated about art because they get more exposure to it. A bit of a circular argument that, I feel. And if exposure to culture makes us more sophisticated, Brian, then why can't we have more of it in the North?

❝ *I felt that all the really important pictures ... should simply be brought down to the South, put in the National Gallery where there are things that go with them, where they would mean more because nothing at all is made of them in the North ... It has to be London-centred. London is where the market is, London is where the great auctioneers are, where the dealers are, so in terms of contemporary art particularly, they need to be here. Working artists need to network with dealers and with curators, they need to be known to the curators of Tate Modern and Tate Britain. They have to be here. They can't be in the Yorkshire Wolds ... It won't work.* **Brian Sewell**

The cheek of it! Not content with what he's already got in London, he wants to import even more and deprive us northerners of the miserably inadequate collections that we have managed to acquire and hang on to. But in one respect, though I hate to admit it, I do think that he's got a point. All the best dealers and curators are concentrated in London so the crucial problem is how can we tempt them away? Because we need people with vision to turn us on. It's all very well having a fantastic building like the Baltic but you'd only go there once or twice to admire the architecture. What it needs (and frequently lacks, I fear) is really stunning art to bring us back there over and over again.

Credit Where Credit's Due

I suppose it's not surprising that London grabs the lion's share of our national art and heritage and then adds to the insult by taking the credit for it all. But even more irritatingly it doesn't stop there. Take pop music for instance – London and the South would even claim the credit for that if we let them.

Well, I don't think London has ever started a pop trend as such. I can't think of one that's ever been started. In the 1960s it was the Liverpool scene, that was the one that got all the attention, fronted, of course, by the Beatles. Every sort of band then wanted to sound like the Beatles. As soon as something comes to London, and it becomes successful, they claim it as their own. They don't claim it came from Birmingham or Manchester or Geordie-land or wherever. They claim that it's come from London. Because probably they signed to a record company that's in London. So London claim it as their own. ***Noddy Holder***

So while we're at it, let's have a roll call of some of the writers and artists who came from the North:

W H Auden
Alfred, Lord Tennyson
Robert Louis Stevenson
Robert Burns
Beatrix Potter
D H Lawrence
William Wordsworth
William Shakespeare
The Brontë Sisters
The Beverley Sisters (sorry, got a bit carried away)
Arnold Bennett
Alan Bennett
J R R Tolkien (a South African by birth, but a Brummie by upbringing)
L S Lowry
Damien Hirst
David Hockney
Sir Henry Moore
Sir Edward Elgar

And where would the world of showbiz be without the sons and daughters of the North? We've even managed a few home-grown toffs of our own.

Dame Judi Dench
Sir Ian McKellen
Sir Nigel Hawthorne
Sir Paul McCartney
Ewan McGregor
Victoria Wood
Les Dawson
Arthur Askey
Ken Dodd
Frank Skinner
Billy Connolly
Jasper Carrott
Lenny Henry
Julie Walters
Alexei Sayle
Johnny Vegas
Peter Kay
Frankie Howerd
Maureen Lipman
Michael Palin
Morecambe and Wise
Stan Laurel
Ant and Dec
Tony Hancock
Meera Syal
Trevor Eve

I could go on all day …

Of course, a nation's art and culture amounts to more

than the stuff you hang on the walls in a gallery or perform in a theatre. If there's one thing that the North has turned into an art form it is going out on the town and having a good time, especially at the weekend. This tradition is for everyone, not just young people intent on hitting the bars and looking for a good time … though the 16–25 age group is responsible for some of the best street theatre you are ever likely to see outside the Edinburgh Festival – and all for free.

“ *I love it when you get little snippets of conversation. When I go back to Liverpool I love walking past and getting sound bites. I heard this girl saying, 'For the life of me I couldn't remember what the Portuguese for blow job was.' There's a bit of culture for you.* ***Kate Robbins***

People in the North just love having a good time, and the weekend generally starts on a Thursday night. They also like a drink – a bit too much. In Merseyside 46 per cent of men and 28 per cent of women exceed the recommended alcohol intake every week and in the northeast 25 per cent of men and 13 per cent of women binge drink on a regular basis.

And Here is the News …

The media is *so* London-centric, it's not true. It will come as no surprise to you to learn that around 90% of programme-makers and decision-makers in the media are based in London. They know sweet FA about real life in the North so when they do portray it they reach for the nearest clichés.

Obviously, the news plays a big part in people's perceptions of the north of England or anywhere outside London. It's ridiculous that you have the six o'clock news and they go, 'Now live to our northern correspondent,' like it's Kate Adie, like they're in some war-torn area ... 'our northern correspondent'. Some bloke in a flak jacket on a council estate in Lancashire going, 'Yes, here I am in the North, it's terrible in the North.' **Justin Moorhouse**

The trouble is, and there's no real point denying it, the national news produced in London is so much better than the local news coming out of the regional TV centres. Have you noticed how they now have that silly phrase, 'Now we go to the news where you are … ' which is code for, 'We're bogging off for a cup of coffee while you all watch paint dry.' Regional broadcasting is still starved of money and resources and it comes across as, well … frankly second-rate and provincial (there's that awful word again).

I've stayed in lots of hotels up and down the country ... you watch the national news and you go, all right, OK, then it switches to the regional news and you get some right dodgy-looking reporter, with one eye going out here, who hasn't been shopping for clothes for a very long time. **Carol Smillie**

On the Street Where You Live

But if ever you doubted the existence of the North–South divide, then take a comparative look at the nation's two favourite soaps: *Coronation Street* and *EastEnders*. They are like chalk and cheese and frankly you come down on one side or the other.

My God, if I have to live either in Coronation Street or adjacent to the Queen Vic public house, I'll take Coronation Street every time. ***Roy Hattersley***

But how realistic is *Corrie*? How true is it to the North these days? It has all gone noticeably up-market. Never mind pork scratchings behind the bar – there's more call for *spaghetti carbonara* these days. The people who live on the Street have all knocked their two downstairs rooms into one to make a 'through lounge', they knock back the Pinot Grigio, and when they knock off work they get Steve McDonald to run them to Manchester Airport and fly off to Ibiza for their holidays.

And I don't like how many people on the programme [Coronation Street] *are essentially simpletons. There aren't that many Elsie Tanners on it any more. If you look at them, to a greater or lesser degree, they're all idiots. No one ever makes a success of anything. Ken Barlow, the one person who ostensibly is supposed to be an intelligent bloke, is a fool, really. He's a fool who's flip-flopped from one job to another, had very disastrous relationships. I can get quite serious about this and think, you know, the only entrepreneur in it is a Cockney.* ***Stuart Maconie***

The Street *is often accused of showing the North as being cloth cap and clogs, the basic side of it. It isn't a true representation of the whole of the North. It is a true representation of that particular social strata ... If everyone thinks that is the North and that's all there is, then they've got it wrong. There's a lot of very high-powered people in big businesses and influential things going on in the North but it doesn't represent a totality of the North.* ***William Roache***

They don't make them like that any more – *Coronation Street*'s gutsy, glamorous Elsie Tanner (Pat Phoenix).

Steady on there, Ken. But the thing about *Corrie* is that – like in the real north – the jokes are better, and in that sense the comparison is a useful one. I'm not saying there are no jokes in the southern rival *EastEnders*, but they seem to go in for gritty conflict and kitchen-sink drama rather than the wry comic spin – why else would Hilda and Stan Ogden have been such comedy icons?

It's Funny Up North

Coronation Street and *EastEnders* have always gone head to head in the ratings war, but surely no sensible person could argue with my opinion that *Corrie* is funnier and the scripts are played for laughs much more. Which is not surprising, since it's a proven fact that we are simply much better at comedy in the North than they are down south.

> " *If you think of northern comedy, OK, there's Bernard Manning and I know he's the bête noire. But if you think Les Dawson, Peter Kay, if you think Alan Bennett, Victoria Wood, the northern comedy, there does seem to be something life-affirming and essentially sympathetic about northern comedy. But if you think about southern comedy, quite often it's kind of ... I mean, Mike Reid and Jim Davidson are two names that spring to mind, and it's all a little bit more brash, isn't it? There's something kind of confrontational and brash and superior about it, based on putting people down a lot more than northern comedy is.*
> ***Stuart Maconie***

We're just better at it. Typical northern comedy as performed by Les Dawson and Roy Barraclough.

There is some truth in this, and when I get a minute I'll do a PhD in it and amuse myself for three years thinking about the comedy roots of some of the funniest and most outrageous comedians in the UK. Look at the Perrier Award winners, for instance. Not many of them come from the South – it seems like the northern way of life is conducive to comedy and jokes, although we did spawn *The Comedians*, which is not much to show off about. It was a series featuring a load of politically incorrect joke-tellers, and I think both Bernard Manning and Roy Chubby Brown are from up our way, so let's move swiftly on …

On Film

The feature film industry is also thriving in the North because film-makers cottoned on to the fact that it's less congested up here and you don't have to stop shooting every five minutes to let the planes go over. They also discovered that the landscapes are stunning, the locals are much more friendly and the catering is cheaper.

But the annoying thing is that London-based TV and film crews are usually so amazed to find themselves in the real north that they invariably feel they have to make it look like the fictional north that exists in the popular imagination. So *plus ça change* …

> *Whenever anyone comes to Wigan to film any kind of report on anything, you would always get that stock shot of smoking chimneys, sooty-faced men walking down cobblestone streets … those kinds of things. And the only way in modern Wigan anyone comes home from work sooty-faced these days is if the photocopier cartridge has broken on them in the office.*
> ***Stuart Maconie***

You know exactly when a film's going to be about the North because the opening scene will be a camera going over a hill and just looking over a mill town and then suddenly some brass band will start playing before you go straight to a scene where it's busy and they're coming out of a factory ... and every single northern film's like that. People must come to Yorkshire from London on a Heartbeat tour and just walk round going, 'But they've got modern cars.' It's all preserved. Yorkshire's preserved for southerners to come and visit to see what people used to live like. ***Justin Moorhouse***

We've got an uphill struggle fighting against the stereotypical images of the North that have come spewing out of our televisions over the years, which all reinforce the clichéd view that the North is gritty, quaint or impoverished in their own way. Here are just a few of them: *Crossroads, Coronation Street, Emmerdale, Brookside, Hollyoaks, Heartbeat, Peak Practice, Our Friends in the North, Fat Friends, Where the Heart Is, All Creatures Great and Small, The Likely Lads, When the Boat Comes In, Auf Wiedersehen Pet, Taggart, Monarch of the Glen, Dr Finlay's Casebook, The Liver Birds, Bread, Brass, The Boys from the Black Stuff, Queer as Folk, Clocking Off, Shameless, 55 Degrees North, Byker Grove, Last of the Summer Wine ...*

I think dramas set in the North have hugely affected the way we think about the North because every time you see a drama based in the North it's on some grotty, awful council estate. Everyone is ugly, they are all poverty-stricken, you know ... you leave your car outside this flat and all the wheels disappear of a night. ***Carole Malone***

On the telly and in films northerners are still cast as down-to-earth, gruff individuals, not multimillionaires, even though – as it happens – we have more than our fair share of those up here. But, as usual, when it comes to the premieres …

Don't get me wrong, I want them to come up here and shoot their films and TV dramas, even ones with Brad Pitt or Mel Gibson. I mean, we can do caravans – sorry, trailers – as well as they can down south. But when it comes to the premieres, guess where they hold them? Even *Billy Elliot*, a film firmly anchored in the northeast, opened 300 miles away in London. They premiered *Calendar Girls*, set in Yorkshire, in London, too. There have been one or two notable exceptions – *Kes*, which was held in Barnsley, and *The Full Monty* in Sheffield, for example – but Leicester is never going to compete with Leicester Square. And I wonder if there is a Hollywood producer fool enough to set foot in Scotland again after the *Braveheart* debacle. Apparently they hired Stirling Castle for the premiere and put on a really lavish do. But the projector broke down and it was left to an embarrassed Mel Gibson to fill in with an impromptu commentary until the problem was fixed. I think that's called shooting yourself in the foot.

Mind you, one advantage of all this is that the North remains a relatively celebrity-free zone. Not for us endless C-list parties where you might be sitting next to Lionel Blair or Clodagh Rogers, not for us bumping into one of the Goodies at the paper shop.

There's no such thing as the paparazzi in Scotland at all … I could run absolutely bollock-naked through the city centre for about an hour and it would never, ever make it in the papers. They're not very quick. **Carol Smillie**

Two Up, Two Down

The arrogance of southerners never ceases to amaze me. They don't even give us credit for having some of the nation's most astonishing architecture. Out of sight, out of mind, as usual. And they think we all live in grimy little houses with a slagheap for a back garden.

To hear southerners talk about northern architecture you would assume that all we've got up here is squalid back-to-backs or ugly pebble-dash semis. Well, I've been to Slough and Chingford and the Elephant and Castle, you know, and let me tell you: no one has a monopoly on the mediocre. Developers don't discriminate and they've blanketed the entire country with their town-centre concrete monstrosities, suburban sprawl and brown-site business parks with no architectural merit whatsoever. What gets me, is that people down south don't realize that we've got buildings in the North that are as graceful and charming as anything they can offer, if not more so. Who would have guessed that there are more fine Georgian buildings in Liverpool than in Bath? And in 2004 Radio 4 listeners voted historic Grey Street in Newcastle (opposite) the most popular street in England.

This Sporting Life

You can't write a chapter about culture in the North without spending a big dollop of time talking about sport. Sport is more than a pastime up here, it's a way of life. Pastimes make you think of stamp-collecting or growing tomatoes, whereas sport, especially football, is a religion. Research has shown that if a home team loses in the northeast then the incidence of heart attacks among the supporters rises

over the next 24 hours. No kidding. You know football is important because when a parliamentary candidate or a minister makes a speech in the run-up to an election in the North they will always include a joke about the local team as they've all been told this is the way to bond with the natives. You could give them a really bad steer by briefing them with the wrong names of some of the players from West Bromwich Albion or Sunderland, and they'd be found out as frauds and southern toffs who only know about cricket or lawn tennis. Tempting, I know.

I remember watching Hugh Grant interviewed before a Cup Final once, about Fulham. Fulham to me represents everything that is johnny-come-lately, Flash Harry, about southern football. Hugh Grant was interviewed as the typical Fulham supporter. I thought, 'Yes that's very accurate.' He said, 'I've been coming to Fulham since 1966. First game I saw was Fulham versus WBA.' 'WBA?' I thought to myself. 'Oh, he means West Brom.' Now there speaks someone who's got into football 25 minutes ago. No one calls them WBA. **Stuart Maconie**

When Sir Bobby Robson was granted the freedom of the city of Newcastle in March 2005 he made a truly awesome speech. He is a god in the northeast, of course. If he took to preaching at Grey's Monument in the city every Sunday morning crowds would gather immediately and queue up to touch his hand and kiss the ground he stood on. Anyway, you get the picture. His acceptance speech put into words an obsession with the beautiful game that is not just reserved for former managers and players – ordinary people really do live and breathe their football in the North.

Bobby Robson told his audience that getting the freedom of the city was more important than his investiture. He paid tribute to the regeneration of the city he loves, saying that he thought the Tyneside quayside development was truly astonishing. He recalled how his father, a miner for 51 years, had been a lifelong supporter of his home team. Till his dying day he had talked about the 1932 Cup Final between Arsenal and Newcastle United, still arguing about whether a crucial goal was offside or not. With a score of Newcastle 2, Arsenal 1, the passion that that historic game aroused in the hearts of the supporters is living proof that the North–South divide is as strong as ever when it comes to football.

The South can keep its cricket and its lawn tennis because everyone knows that we invented football in the North and football is the only game that matters. And it matters all over the world. OK, so the first game of football ever played was at Westminster School but you get the idea, and in any case it's our turn to get the credit for something. Britain's oldest football club is Sheffield FC and it's where the first ever rule book for the game was produced, in 1857. The first professional football league was set up in 1888 in Manchester, at the Royal Hotel in Piccadilly.

WE STARTED FOOTBALL

– I've put this in large, capital letters, just in case you didn't get it.

You know you're in the cradle of the game once you come north and see some of the names that are to football what the shipping forecast is to fishermen: Crewe Alexandra, Tranmere Rovers, Halifax Town, Blackburn, Liverpool, Bury, Wolverhampton Wanderers, Accrington Stanley … These wonderful northern football clubs read like a lesson in geography of the North. Southern names never roll off the tongue in quite the same way: Sevenoaks, Guildford, Slough, Maidstone … no, it doesn't do it for me.

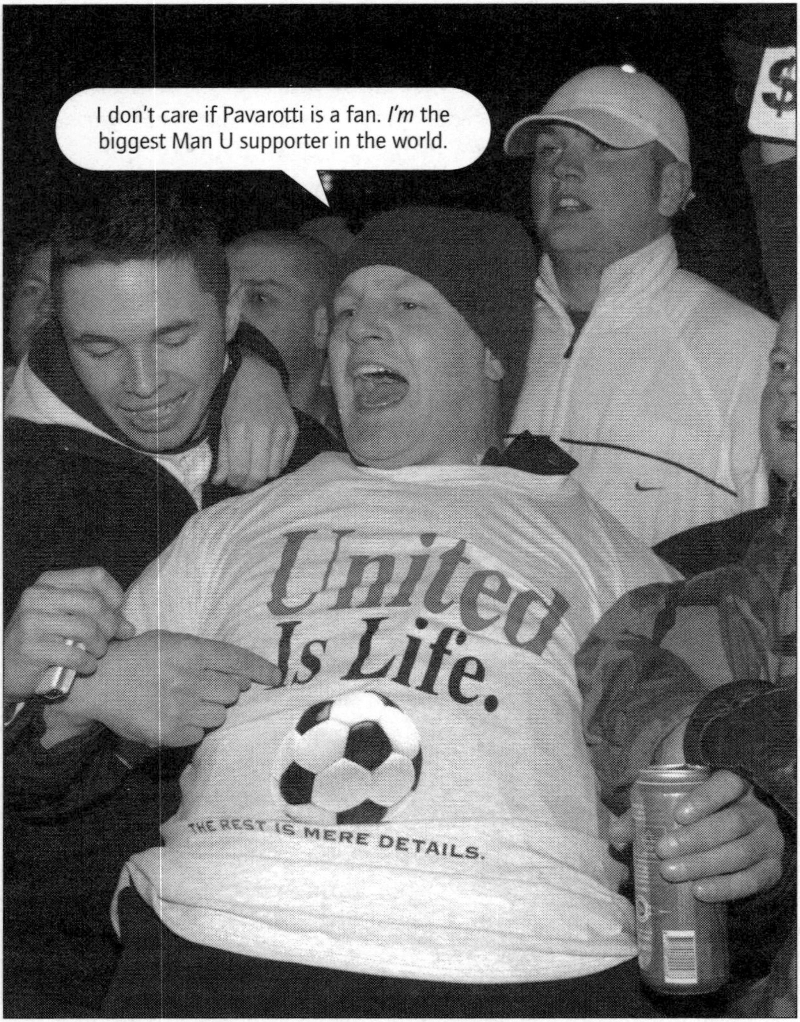

The most famous football club in the world. Man U has a huge following in the South. Can't you find a good enough team down there, then?

It is fantastically evocative. And football always helps geography. I remember someone asking once when I was about twelve, 'Where's Carlisle?' And I said, 'About halfway up the first division, isn't it?' 'Cos I just assumed that's what they meant. ***Stuart Maconie***

Many northern teams are so superior that they have as many honorary supporters from the South as they do from the North. There are evidently more Man U supporters down south than there are up north. You'd expect the ex-pats from the North who have had to move to London to get jobs to support their teams but where do all the others come from?

But quite frankly, it's a well-known fact that Manchester United ... the bulk of the fans don't come from Manchester, they come from all over the rest of the world, and a lot of Manchester United fans come from the South. So they can't find a good team in the South, can they, to support; they have to come north to find a good team. ***Noddy Holder***

The football thing is quite interesting. In the North you are defined by your team and what you support and it always makes me laugh ... why so many Londoners support Man U. The reason, I would imagine, is that no team in London has ever been successful (apart from Arsenal) in the last 20–25 years. Every team that's won anything has been from the north of England or the Midlands. ***Justin Moorhouse***

Perhaps we should point out, by the way, that Arsenal is in *north* London. Mind you, Chelsea isn't north London and they do pretty well … they must have a big north stand, then. We can cope with southerners idolizing our teams but now they've started mucking about with the game itself.

In the last 10 or 15 years I think there has been a kind of gentrification and to that extent a southernification (if there's such a word) of football. As you know, it's a working-class game but I think there has been what Roy Keane would call the 'prawn sandwichification' of football. And it has all rather become horribly glossy and corporate. **Stuart Maconie**

So on the whole we blame the South and the southern influence on our game for making it such big business and turning the whole process of getting to the match on a Saturday into such a pain, and more to the point, making it so criminally expensive. All supporters want to buy their team's latest strip but the clubs are ripping them off by changing the designs every five minutes. This is definitely 'prawn sandwichification' and to be honest, it stinks.

The other thing that stinks is the decision to rebuild the new national football stadium at Wembley. What a missed opportunity. It's obvious that Birmingham should have got the venue. London has already got national stadiums for rugby, tennis and cricket at Twickenham, Wimbledon and Lords, so why not break the habit of a lifetime and give something back to the loyal football fans in the North? After all, we've been using the Millennium Stadium in Cardiff for the internationals ever since Wembley Stadium shut down, but oh no, the Londoners have been whingeing about the inconvenience of getting to South Wales. You see … give them a taste of their own medicine and they don't like it.

Oh, you put those football phone-ins on and you're always getting people – not just Arsenal supporters and Chelsea supporters – and they're going, 'You won't believe the traffic here, mate, it's taken us seven hours.' Well, now you know what it feels like when our teams got to the FA Cup Final every year and we had to go to Wembley. I don't think our national stadium should have been in London. I think even a London-based planner with some common sense and a map and ruler might have worked out that somewhere near Junction 3 of the M5 might have been a good place for a national stadium. I mean, having it where it is at Wembley is about as sensible as having it in Aberdeen, really. ***Stuart Maconie***

They're rebuilding Wembley Stadium. It's always been a pain to get to – you could never park or get to it through the traffic or on public transport. Impossible. And what do they do? They start to rebuild it all over again. They've learned no lessons whatsoever – they're putting it back up in exactly the same place. Why not put it in the Midlands, so everybody all around the country can get to it easily? You know, there's big wide open spaces there. There's rail, there's airports ... do they think we're still living in the Dark Ages? ***Noddy Holder***

With all these controversies raging within the game, the gloves are now off. The old stereotype of the gritty northerner versus the lily-livered southern bastards endures even when half the players are no longer British. Man U's Alex Ferguson has no time for what he calls 'Chelsea's effete bunch of mercenaries' – even if they are Britain's most expensive player squad.

What does Chelsea do? It gets a Russian billionaire and it buys stars from another world. The northern way of doing it is to bring up people in the game in the proper way ... it's a big distinction, a big difference. ***Roy Hattersley***

We won't mention the name Malcolm Glazer though …

It's Just Not Cricket

Cricket is another matter entirely. It is a game that when it's played in the North is at a distinct disadvantage, because the weather is cloudier and wetter up here. With cricket, rain stops play, and time lost for bad weather is lost forever, so southern teams are more likely to win because they get more practice and their games are less susceptible to interruption. To explain in more detail, let me call on Dr Alan Hignall, who has written a fascinating and – how shall I put it? – painstaking book on this very subject, called … *Rain Stops Play.*

Lancashire have not won the County Championship outright since 1934. Since then the counties in the south-east have won 27 championships – Surrey have won 11, Kent 2, Essex 6, Middlesex 7 and Sussex 1. Between 1998 and 2004 Lancashire lost 328.25 hours of playing time at home in County Championship matches – the equivalent of roughly 13 matches. In the same time period, the weather being considerably better down south, Surrey lost only 218.5 hours (8.5 matches), Kent 236 hours (9.5 matches), Essex 202 hours (8 matches), Middlesex 227.75 hours (9 matches), and Sussex 133 hours (5 matches). The County Championship consists in theory of 16 matches (8 home and 8 away) and it turns out that because of bad weather Lancashire lost the equivalent of one entire Championship match at home each year, so this represents a serious handicap when compared with counties in the southeast. I could go on and analyse Yorkshire's cricket record but I don't want to bore you and I am already in danger of losing the will to live. But you get the general idea … I hope.

Despite these disadvantages, the North has produced

more than its fair share of sporting heroes. And by a happy coincidence they are more likely to come from Lancashire than any other part of England, according to a survey that the Barclays 'Spaces for Sports' carried out in February 2005. Their sporting map records the birthplaces of 500 men and women with the highest number of international caps in the past 100 years in football, Rugby Union, Rugby League, athletics, cricket and netball. Lancashire produced 14% of the people on the list across all the sports and 19% of the leading footballers. Yorkshire can take heart, though, because they have produced more cricketing heroes than anywhere else.

So it seems that the North continues its cultural dominance in two important arenas – football and going out of a Friday night and getting, as they say up here, 'bladdered'. But the message is: we want more art and culture up here than we have at the moment and, funnily enough, I think you'll find that once it comes – as surely it will – us northerners will make sure we make the most of it.

CHAPTER SEVEN

Food

What do southerners know about northern food? They're probably daft enough to think Pontefract cakes and barm cakes are cakes. Southerners can't even sprinkle vinegar on their chips straight from the bottle properly; they have to use one of those silly tops with a little hole in, and they also use a daft wooden fork – really! As if we needed evidence of our superiority! Mind you, we northerners have no time for their food fads down south. If sushi bars took off in Sunderland they'd probably have to offer all the raw fish you can eat for a fiver, because up north we like good food and we like a lot of it too.

The Fat of the Land

Which might explain why northerners tend to be … well, bigger. Yes, I admit, we northerners *do* occasionally eat some things that are bad for us and yes, we probably *do* weigh more (collectively) than southerners. But we're sick of them going on and on at us for eating lard and pies. If we want a bag of chips with scraps and a battered saveloy *and* some deep-fried pineapple rings for afters (you need a doctor's note, mind), then we'll have them, thank you very much. Just leave us alone to get on with it.

Deep-fried Mars bars – they've become legendary. I have never seen one, I don't know anyone that's seen one in Scotland, but I don't know a chippie in Glasgow that wouldn't serve you a deep-fried pizza. ***Carol Smillie***

They'd probably arrest you down south for asking for one of those.

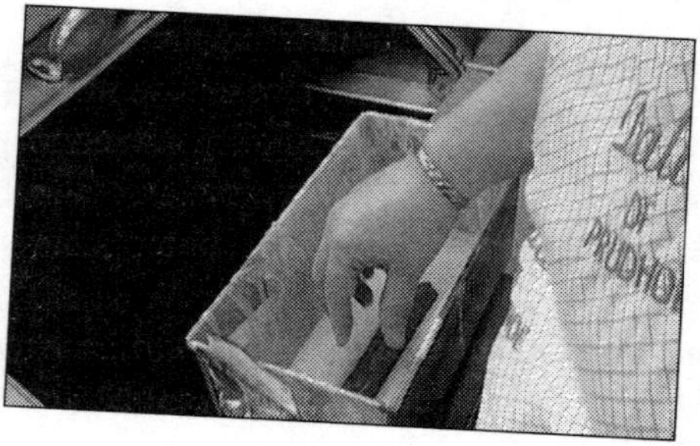

'Now, take your freshly peeled Mars bar and dip it gently into the batter ... '

Data analysts Experian published a survey in 2004 that, I have to reveal, says that the fattest towns (those with the chubbiest people) in England are all in the North:

1 Hull, Humberside
2 Knowsley, Merseyside
3 Blackburn, Lancashire
4 South Tyneside
5 Easington, County Durham

It will come as no surprise that the top five leanest towns were all in London or Greater (or do I mean Smaller?) London:

1 Kingston-on-Thames
2 Kensington and Chelsea
3 Westminster
4 Richmond
5 Wandsworth

In the same year, a men's fitness magazine declared that the top five fattest cities were:

1 Manchester
2 Stoke-on-Trent
3 Liverpool/Swansea
5 Leicester

The previous year Glasgow was the fattest city, so they can't be eating as many deep-fried pizzas there as they used to.

Londoners are indeed skinnier than people in the North. They eat less meat and more fruit than anyone else, which is good. Bizarrely, they also have the lowest percentage of microwaves per household. I find this hard to believe because they are big on kettle snacks, i.e. things you cook with the kettle, like pot noodles and so on (no surprises as to where most of those are consumed … but let's not tell everyone that). I guess it's more likely that they must have switched to pan-frying or lightly grilling all their meals. I am pleased to announce, though, that while southerners' diets may be healthier, it is recorded that Londoners suffer from more flatulence than anyone else. I couldn't have put it better myself.

But if we're talking the southern health police here then I would like to remind them that we're not the ones who are stressed out by working 14-hour days; we're not the ones who make do with half an hour for lunch day after day; we're not the ones who can't afford the time to take paternity leave (men) or have a baby and so take maternity leave (women); we're not the ones who take their mobiles – sorry BlackBerrys – on holiday and phone the office every morning. I could go on … Messrs Holland and Barrett would bear me out because their sales figures for 2003 show that Londoners buy more energy-enhancing supplements than the rest of us. So they must feel the need for a bit of a boost, poor things.

Anyway, I don't accept the criticism of the southern fitness fascists because the food in the North is fantastic. I don't just mean the chips and pies and puddings, although we do those definitively well, but everything else, too. And we don't all eat meat, you know. The Reverend William Cowherd first started to preach the new doctrine of vegetarianism in Salford way back in 1809 (presumably as a way of diverting attention from his unfortunate surname) and the Vegetarian Society held its first meeting in Manchester in 1848. We have the finest culinary traditions. Southerners have no idea about all the cheeses and fresh fruit and veg, a lot of it organic, that we produce in the North.

Look at the results of the Organic Food Awards in 2004 – the organic business person of the year, Gordon Tweddle, runs the Acorn Organic Dairy in County Durham, one of the best organic meat producers is in Northumberland, and Woodlands Farm in Kirton in Lincolnshire has a list of prizes as long as your arm for their organic veggies. And the organic trophy for lifetime achievement went to a couple growing veggies for their box scheme in Pilling in Lancashire. So you don't have to live in Somerset or Wiltshire these days to get some truly fabulous organic food.

..ere are just some of the foods we make or grow in the North that are the best in their field:

- Smoked salmon from Shropshire
- Bread – Melmerby Organic Bakery near Penrith is astonishingly good and exports masses of its stunning organic bread down to the deep south – I was in Glastonbury recently and saw some of their bread on sale – because it is so fantastic (so much for northern food being a load of stodgy cheap pies)
- Organic food – there are dozens of brilliant organic farm shops that are springing up in the North, one of the best being Low Sizergh Barn in Cumbria, just off Junction 36 of the M6. They've lost count of how many awards they've won, but I know they won Best Tea Shop of 2004 in *Period Living and Traditional Homes* magazine. They had 100,000 visitors last year, who bought some of their fantastic organic produce and watched the cows being milked through an ingenious glass panel – this takes place most days at 3.30–3.45 p.m.
- Cartmel sticky toffee – the stunning village of Cartmel in Cumbria is a wonderful village with a twelfth-century priory, a market square with a babbling brook running through it and an astonishing Michelin-starred restaurant in the form of L'Enclume. The local sticky toffee pudding is a phenomenon not to be missed – you'd be well advised to stock up with as much of it as your boot will take. The Johns family started making it in The Village in 1984 and it became so popular that they grew out of the kitchen there, spread out into kitchens all over the village, including converted garages, and now they export all over the country and have had to build a plant in Flookburgh to keep up with the demand in 300 outlets,

including Waitrose (down south) – they even have a branch in Santa Monica, California now. Marvellous!

- Earl Grey tea – this originated in Newcastle and was named after a man who lived there. Who'd have thought hairdressers' tea would have come from a place so awash with builders?

Now that's what I call a claim to fame.

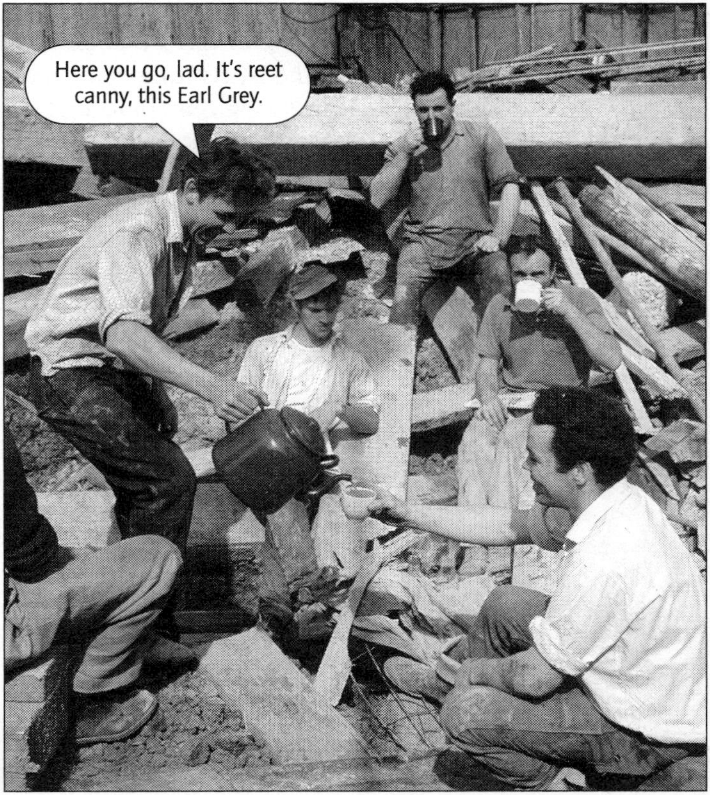

The Chip on Our Shoulder

Let's start the debate proper with the one thing that you can't argue with, even if you live in Essex: northern chips are officially better than anywhere else in the world. Sadly, I have to exclude the honorary north from this discussion. I grant you, the Cornish are wonderful fishermen and what they don't know about things that live in the sea is not worth knowing, but chips? They're out of their league.

❝ *The meal that I miss the most from the northeast is fish and chips. We used to go to North Shields to the fish quay and you get fish and chips in the paper with mushy peas and loads of sauce and vinegar – the brown vinegar, not the nancy white vinegar – and we would go and sit on the fish quay and look at the water where the fish had come out just 24 hours before. And that was all for about £2.50. So that is the thing that I miss the most. That feeling, that taste of those fish. It's not the same on a plate in a restaurant. That's not chips. Chips are done in lard, lots of nice lard, and then you get the little bits of crispy crackling and everything, which are horribly full of fat and carbohydrate, but hell, who cares?* ***Carole Malone***

❝ *Fish and chips and mushy peas, yes, and lots of vinegar – not balsamic, proper malt vinegar. You can't have these fancy vinegars on your chips – it's got to be home malt vinegar. And if they sold good pickled onions, which they usually did, you had a couple of them as well.* ***Noddy Holder***

❝ *Mind you, I do still have a thing about mushy peas. I do like mushy peas. We'll have fish and chips down south sometimes and I'll just have a portion of mushy peas. But mushy peas then were the ones that you soaked over night. You got them*

in a packet and they were hard and you put them in a large bowl of water with one of them tablets which looked like Alka Seltzer … I was never sure what was in it. And my dad would do it the night before, on a Saturday night for Sunday dinner, and we'd soak the dried peas over night and then they cooked them the following day. And they weren't in a tin or in a polystyrene carton stuck in a microwave. It was an industry, cooking these dried peas.
Alan Titchmarsh

The British fish and chips industry is big business and it's worth £650 million a year. There are some 12,000 fish and chip shops in the UK, as opposed to 1250 outlets of McDonald's, so that's a lot more chippies than McDonald's. So there is a God. It's the country's most popular meal.

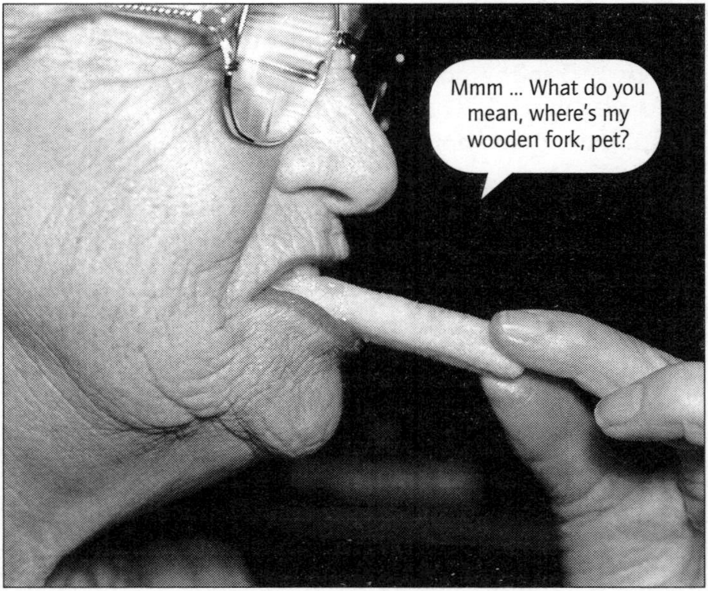

People in the Midlands eat the most (27 million portions in 2003) and the northwest comes second (23.6 million) with London not far behind (20 million).

Lancashire saw the birth of the very first fish and chip shop, which opened for business near Oldham in 1863. They also sold pigs' trotters in batter, which were probably enough to scare small children and give the rest of us nightmares – no wonder they went out of fashion. We're told that there are now four times as many fish and chip shops in Lancashire than in the whole of London. So Lancashire now has the highest ratio of chip shops to people – there is one for every 900 potential customers. In London you would have to queue for quite a long time, because each chippy there has to serve a population of 22,727.

Perhaps the most famous chippy in the world is Harry Ramsden's, which has been serving the people of Guiseley in West Yorkshire since 1928, and now has an astonishing 112 outlets in the UK.

In praise of the northern chip …

" *The northern chip is a big chip, it's the kind of chip that if you drop one you've actually lost something. If you drop a southern chip what have you lost? You've lost a tiny little thing, what's the big deal? A big northern chip lands on the floor, you can hear it, and I like that in a chip.* ***Jenny Eclair***

Did you know that the average big, chunky northern chip is supposedly much healthier for you than the skinny ones that they serve up at McDonald's? This is because the smaller the chip, the greater the ratio of fat to potato.

In the South I discovered when I came here 40 years ago, they actually buy chips in a chip shop and eat them with little wooden forks. Well, chips were designed to be eaten with your fingers and chips were designed to be sprinkled with salt and vinegar. I suspect there are some people in the South who don't know how to sprinkle vinegar, which requires a very, very careful half-application of the thumb over the top so it sprinkles over the thumb, and there some people in the South that I suspect can't even do that. ***Roy Hattersley***

Even Michael Winner conceded we win at chips:

I must say if you go to fish and chip shops in the North, as I have done, because the food is otherwise so awful, they're normally very, very good. There's a fish and chip shop in Manchester, the chips were fantastic, you could see they were cut on the premises, they were different shapes, they were different sizes. The fish was excellent, the batter was excellent. I think the commoner you can be in the North the more chance you have of eating a good meal.
Michael Winner

Even in a chippy it's easy to fool the enemy, though. I imagine if Michael Winner saw scallops on the menu in Barnsley he'd be right impressed. But he wouldn't know what a scallop was. Not a real one.

A scallop in the North is a thin sliver of potato fried in batter. Of course, if you're Marco Pierre White or Gordon Ramsay, a scallop is something very different. So it's always fun when you see scallops on a northern chippy board. And we sometimes call them a smack as well. So that would make them even more excited, wouldn't it? Scallops and smack: 25p.
Stuart Maconie

Lard-Di-Da

Real northern chips are fried in beef dripping or lard. They don't appreciate this down south and I've even heard a rumour that they cook their chips in olive oil, though I have no proof. Did you know there is a world shortage of lard? Yes, a world shortage. It was in such short supply pre-Christmas 2004 that someone started to stock-pile it and put it up for auction on eBay. The reason for this national crisis is because people in countries like Hungary and Poland have started to buy up all our cheaper cuts of pork. And because they are now part of the EEC they no longer have to pay import duty. We used to render this meat into lard but now the East Europeans are taking it all because they don't mind if their bacon is really streaky as long as the price is right. Hence the shortage. And when commodities are in short supply we all have to pay more. And what will that do to the price of fish?

Paul Heathcote, the restaurateur who owns the Simply Heathcote and Olive Press chain, reckons that lard has become more popular because people are going back to the old-fashioned style of English cooking. At last southerners have woken up to the fact that roast potatoes, pasties and steam puddings taste infinitely better when they're made with lard as they always used to be. So now there is a rush for it. It's time to stash a load away in the cellar and then we can flog it all back to them down south at £10 a pack. Tell them it's organic. They'll go for that. The Lard Marketing Board has its own website (www.zen8595.zen.co.uk/lard), which offers quite the most entertaining five minutes spent in polite company that I can remember in a while. Their T-shirts are simply to die for.

They're young... They're in love...
They eat LARD

Not only is lard better on flavour, it apparently has fewer calories than butter: one tablespoon contains 13 grams of fat, 116 calories and 12 milligrams of cholesterol. Plus the Italians eat it, so that's another reason why southerners are taking it seriously. They call it *lardo di colonnata*, which is quite the rage among cookery writers and chefs over here as well as there. It's heavily seasoned and is a delicacy of the Apuane Mountains. They send specially trained dogs to sniff it out and dig it out of the earth for them while they take relaxed lunches alfresco and chill out. Either that or they buy it at their equivalent of Spar, which is probably called Spar anyway.

Portion Control

Apart from chips, what else do we like up north? The first thing to say is that we like a lot of it, whatever it is. Size matters. As with so many other things, southerners have managed to interfere with our notion of portions big time (or do I mean small time?). In the North we like a nice big plate of food in front of us. We are not fooled by their mealy-mouthed ways down south. They do give you a nice big plate, granted, but then they put a tiny mound of food in the middle, like it's meant to be artistic or something. And then they have the cheek to charge you £20 when all you are getting is a couple of spoonfuls. In the North, if we're eating out, we want our money's worth. We don't want to have to stop at the chippy on the way home to tide us over till the morning, we want to have to loosen our trousers or have a lie down.

❝ *If you go to a posh restaurant in London and you order chips you'll get six and then there'll be a small piece of fish on the top and that will be your fish and chips. Oh, how ironic. If you want value, just get in the car and drive North. OK, you might spend 80 quid on petrol, but you'll get that back in your portion size.* **Jenny Eclair**

❝ *I remember when I first came to London and I was in a restaurant and I ordered sea bream. And I got a piece of sea bream that was about four inches by five inches. And I said to the guy, 'No, I asked for a sea bream, not a bit of sea bream, not an eighth of a sea bream.' And he looked at me and he probably spat in it but at least I did get a much bigger piece of fish. I can't get over the portion sizes here, you know, all the time I complain. I send stuff back.* **Carole Malone**

Northerners are born with an in-built inability to leave anything at all on their plates. This is because it is drummed into us from within the womb that wasting food is one of the seven deadly sins. When I was a child the school dinner lady could spot any uneaten food left on a plate at 20 paces. She would stand over us until we ate up every last scrap of fat, gristle, waterlogged cabbage, custard skin … telling us to think of all the starving children in Africa who would give their right arms for even half the amount that we were being so faddy about. Northern dinner ladies are a scary breed. You don't mess with them. We would willingly have shipped all of our overboiled greens and tapioca pudding over to Ethiopia but this was never an option.

Northern women are past masters of the technique of stopping good food from going to waste. 'Waste not, want not' being the general motto. Generations of mothers have been feeding their families economically by preparing a roast on a Sunday, serving the meat cold on a Monday (useful because this was washing day so the kitchen would be full of damp laundry and there was no time to cook anyway) and mincing it up for a shepherd's pie on a Tuesday. By Friday you were reduced to eating bread and dripping for supper until you could afford to start all over again with a proper meal.

“ *You know where you are with a northern mother, and what I mean by 'northern mother' is a woman that goes everywhere by coach, doesn't believe in sell-by dates and can make a chicken last a fortnight. My mother can, you know. She'll get a chicken and she'll roast it, she'll curry it, she'll make enough sandwiches for a wake, and just when you think you can't get any more off that chicken, she'll boil the bones down to make wallpaper paste.* ***Jenny Eclair***

I think it was Wallis Simpson, the Duchess of Windsor, who said that one could never be too rich or too thin, but she was an American and we don't buy that in the North. Up here we have the same attitude that a lot of tribal communities in the world have, namely that looking well fed is a sign of wealth and status in the community. If you look scrawny, then it means you're poor and can't afford to eat well. It's one step away from rickets and bow legs. Either that or you've got a rotten mother who can't cook. Down south, though, scrawny is a desirable look, they'll pay a fortune at some health farm for scrawny. Though if you took all their money off them, they wouldn't be able to afford to eat and that would achieve the same result without it costing them a penny, wouldn't it? It comes from California, you know, this idea that emaciation is a good thing. Once a fad starts in LA you can bet your bottom dollar it'll be on the next flight to London and before you know it we're all into floatation tanks or energizing crystal techniques. You could probably launch a new range of ready meals in LA called Scrawny and they would sell like … well, people on a diet don't eat hot cakes, but you know what I mean.

The pressure to be thin these days is so great and the health lobby so persuasive that traditional northern portion sizes are seriously under threat. If we're not careful we're going to end up as anxious and neurotic about food as the average southerner with their endless eating dilemmas – is it fat-free? Sugar-free? Organic? Low-carb? Or just plain low-fun? Sometimes I think they don't do good old-fashioned common sense down south any more. I mean, no one's stupid enough to eat fish and chips seven days a week, are they? No need to feel suicidal just because you didn't stick to the rules for a day or two. Just get some pies in and get on with it. Obviously, it's no good eating just pies, you have to have the leeks and potatoes as well, but what's wrong with that?

Who Eats All the Pies?

It's time we had a serious talk about pies. I mean proper pies – not filo pastry parcels or samosas or salmon and broccoli quiches, or fancy fish dishes with a bit of mashed potato on top. I'm talking about a serious pork pie, for example, with a heavy pastry bottom to it that would do good service as a doorstop on a windy day. Pies like this were introduced to the north of England by itinerant Irish Catholic priests in the twentieth century, so that they could travel, preach and eat at the same time. Impress your friends with that one – it might come up in a game of Trivial Pursuit one day and you'll feel smug knowing the answer.

Wigan is the pie capital of the world. We take our pies very, very seriously. Pies in general in the North are enjoyed because we're busy people, we've got things to do, they're things you can eat on the move. They're things you can eat at the bus stop. ***Stuart Maconie***

Wigan was the first northern town to take to pies in a big way. The town is associated with pies and pasties that were traditionally very popular with coal miners in the area. Wiganers are often called 'pie eaters' and it has been suggested that this name arose because miners who were out on strike were forced back to work and made to eat humble pie.

The idea of pie-eating soon caught on and it was not long before every miner in the North took one down the pit for their dinner. They were originally called 'coffins', which is quite apt because that is where you'll end up if you eat too many.

We need to establish the technical parameters of something as important as a northern pie. First of all, it's got to have a top on it, so quiches and tartlets are out, and it's got to have a bottom. If all it's got is a top then strictly speaking it's a hotpot. Secondly, it's got to have meat in it. Please note: no fish. What we really need is a bit of simple government legislation to sort this confusion once and for all. We've got to do something to stop people down south from mucking about with our pie heritage.

Clever, eh? Northerners account for over 70% of the nation's entire pie consumption.

You go to a pub down here and they say you can have steak and kidney pie for your lunch. I like steak and kidney pie, we do like pies, northerners, don't know why. Steak and kidney pie comes and it'll be very nice but it won't be a proper pie. It'll be a bowl and there will be a kind of fluffy puff pastry crust on the top and you take that off and there's just meat swirling around in gravy. That's not a pie. That's stew with puff pastry over the top. It's not a pie. A pie has pastry and preferably shortcrust under-

neath it. That proper sort of greasy pork pie. I don't eat them now, you know, cholesterol, but oh, I did love them then.
Alan Titchmarsh

Incidentally, pasties aren't pies, strictly speaking, though they are often as big and filling and good. Since we have already agreed that Cornwall is part of the honorary north, I think their famous pasties should be classified as honorary pies. But I did not include them in the pie chart because that would have ruined the joke … whoever heard of a pasty chart?

Interestingly, data shows a pie-eating cluster, a sort of pie pile-up, in our award-winning fat town – Hull – which just happens to be John Prescott's constituency. Say no more …

What have they to offer, say, in London? I know there used to be a lot of pie and mash places in east London, but I haven't seen one for a while. I'm not even sure they still exist and I'm even less sure how good the southern equivalent would be.

Puddings are always a great source of confusion to people down south. They don't really get them, not the savoury kind, anyway. Say 'pudding' to a southerner and they think you're offering them a nice apple crumble or something.

A great delicacy of the North is the steak pudding. And I remember the first time going to a London chippy and saying, 'Can I have pudding and chips, please?' – and this bloke looking at me, obviously like I was mental. 'Pudding and chips?' 'Yeah, please, pudding and chips and gravy.' He was obviously thinking, like, 'Sticky toffee pudding or a Christmas pudding on some chips?' like I was a complete nutcase. ***Stuart Maconie***

I went into the chip shop in London. You can't get a steak pudding, you know, it's just a suet pudding with steak and kidney, known in some parts of the country as a baby's head, but you can't get those, that's funny, isn't it? That's never made it to the South. I mean, it probably doesn't sound terribly appealing, there's probably people in the South thinking, 'And thank God for that,' you know. It hardly qualifies as a gastronomic desert because we haven't got steak puddings south of the Watford Gap but I like steak pudding. ***Mark Radcliffe***

A Load of Tripe

We in the North are doing a damned decent job of resisting southern influences in all sorts of areas but I have to confess that food is proving to be something of a weak spot. Southerners steal our food, ponce it about a bit and then sell it back to us at ten times the price. If he'd have thought of it, it's the kind of trick that Damien Hirst would have been proud of.

You buy tripe in London now and they serve it in sliver slices and they charge a fortune. Black pudding ... we would eat in the North for breakfast and stuff. Now that is on all the big menus in all the big restaurants for dinner. It's interesting how times have changed. Fish and chips, our staple diet, that is in all London restaurants now and they charge you 17 quid for it. In the North they would laugh at Jamie Oliver, who is charging 15 quid for beans on toast – or beans on ciabatta. People in the North would think you had gone mental to pay £15 for beans on toast but in the South we do. ***Carole Malone***

They do the same with all our rhubarb, parsnips and gooseberries now. There's barely a home-grown savoy cabbage or beetroot to be had up north any more as it all gets whisked away down to London where it's fashioned into something improbable on a plate in a swanky restaurant.

And talking of swanky restaurants – we have some, actually we have quite a lot, but what about being a bit fairer about distributing the all-important Michelin stars, or sending out influential restaurant critics to the North a bit more to write about them in the newspapers? There are 120 restaurants in the UK currently with Michelin stars – and London alone has 35. The South excluding London has 39, and the rest are distributed fairly thinly in the North and the honorary north. Greater Manchester doesn't have one, but there is one now in Altringham, and Birmingham made it for the first time in 2005 with two – Jessica's and Simpsons. The Lakes are relatively well placed for Michelin stars, but nothing like they deserve – two Cumbrian restaurants got two new stars this year – the Samling and L'Enclume – joining Holbeck Ghyll at Windermere, and Sharrow Bay. Cumbria is the only county other than Hampshire to have as many Michelin stars. I haven't had the opportunity to sample them all, but L'Enclume in Cartmel is astonishing. Positively the most imaginative culinary experience I've ever had. Some of the food arrived on a piece of local slate, which accounts for the local roofing contractors doing a roaring trade. And it would be so much more expensive in London. Holbeck Ghyll is one of the other astonishing things in the North that rivals anything you could find in London or the South but is probably a great deal better value for money. The view over the lake and fells is picture postcard, and their Michelin-starred *amuse bouches*, which is one of my favourite over-the-top culinary expressions, knock the spots off Kendal Mint Cake. It can even boast that it's one of the most romantic hotels in the world, according to one American journalist who went there recently and refused to leave. Ever.

Best Thing Since Sliced Bread

Southerners are so hopeless when it comes to food, they don't even know the proper names for something as simple as a bread roll.

❝ *It's a north-south thing. Like baps, which of course has a slightly humorous innuendo quality as well, and cobs. When we were young we used to have bread cobs and we also used to sweat cobs ... weird, eh? So if you were really hot you would say, 'I'm sweating cobs,' but a lump of bread was a bread cob. In the South it was always a roll. In Jersey a biscuit was a bread roll or cob or bap. And then there's 'barm', which doesn't particularly translate. A barm cake is a bap, we used to call them flour cakes. But you know, if you go down south and ask for a barm, they'll give you something to put on your lips. 'I'll have a bacon barm.' 'No, we've got mint flavour, I think we've got grape, we might have strawberry. Bacon balm. Have we got any bacon balm? No, we don't do those.' So there's a big language divide there.* ***Mark Radcliffe***

❝ *A bap in the South is a breast, you see, but in the North it's a floury white roll. A bit similar to what my breasts are like, actually.* ***Jenny Eclair***

Southerners call our pikelets 'crumpets', and our stotties 'bread rolls', and anything that remotely resembles a cake, a muffin. I can't see the point of muffins. Because they add a couple of blueberries they seem to think we are happy to pay about £1.50 a pop. You can keep your muffins. We were happy with cake. Was Marie Antoinette a northerner?

Everything these days has to be Italian or French or Mexican or Chinese. It's wonderful to have the choice but sometimes all you want is a good old stand-by, like a traditional ploughman's lunch with a lump of cheddar, a hunk of crusty white bread and a side order of Branston's. Sometimes you can't even get an ordinary English sandwich. What do they offer you? A baguette? A bagel? An enchilada? A pitta bread wrap? Ciabatta, focaccia … ?

" *If there's one thing that I'd really go to task with London about it's food. Because of London and their swanky ways, you can't get a ham-and-cheese toastie. That used to be the staple for any pub grub, the ham-and-cheese toastie, which was two slices of bread done in the toastie with ham and cheese. Now it's paninis and it costs you three quid more. You can't get a cup of tea, you can't get a cup of coffee, it has to be frothy or have extra milk in it or a shot of this or ... I just want some toast and a cup of tea. And now everywhere in the North is the same. Panini this, panini that. Bruschetta? Bruschetta is toast with tomatoes on and it's £4.95. That's rubbish, isn't it?* ***Justin Moorhouse***

And what have they done with our sweet trolley? Where has all the Black Forest gateau gone? And our prawn cocktails and our chilli con carnes, come to think of it – we used to like them. I'll tell you what's happened. These dishes have gone out of fashion in the South so no one's allowed to have them any more. They're considered too white trash so the southern food monitors have confiscated them all.

The food in the North is, by and large, beyond belief, terrible. They write these menus in this flowery language and you know there is nobody in the kitchen that could achieve anything remotely like it. And the menu is enormous, so not only do you have these very complicated dishes described normally with spelling mistakes all over them, but there are hundreds of them. And there is some twit in the kitchen, if he could do a fried egg, lovely, I'll have a fried egg. Fried egg and beans, marvellous. But you don't get the northern dishes – Lancashire hotpot and this sort of thing, which are magnificent, you get this ponced-about, supposedly French, third-rate – not third-rate, hundredth-rate – photocopy that is usually uneatable. ***Michael Winner***

OK, so we don't have the Ivy, or Le Gavroche, or Langhams and personally I can think of a million and one things I would rather do with the £40 they would presumably charge for my tea. Or do I mean my supper? No, I mean my dinner … Oh God, see how confusing southerners have made it for us!

What's in a Name?

Not content with nicking our culinary secrets, southerners insist that the very terms we use for our meals are wrong. The North–South divide leads to a lot of confusion.

It wasn't until I was about 18 and I went to London with work for the first time and they said, 'We're going to take you out for dinner.' So about one o clock I was sat there waiting for them and I rang them up and said, 'I thought we were going out for dinner.' And they went, 'Yes, seven o'clock, mate.' 'What, for your dinner?' I really didn't know. And they were, like, 'We're not having tea.' They thought that was three o'clock, sandwiches at the

Ritz and everything. I think dinner sounds nicer than lunch, anyway. I have my dinner at 12, my tea at five o'clock, and my supper about eight o'clock ... then a snack about 11. ***Justin Moorhouse***

I'm starting to realize why northerners are a bit chubbier ...

My wife is from Hampshire and she would call dinner 'supper'. 'What are you talking about, supper?' She said, 'I'm going to invite some people, you know, I'm going to invite them for supper.' I said, 'You can't invite them for supper, that's ridiculous.' She said, 'What do you mean, you can't invite them for supper?' 'You don't invite people round at half ten, eleven o'clock at night.' She said, 'What are you talking about?' I said, 'No, supper is what you have before you go to bed.' Supper is like cheese on toast at eleven or something or a few digestive biscuits – that's supper. ***Mark Radcliffe***

Before southerners started messing about with it all, it was very simple. You had three meals a day: your breakfast, your dinner and your tea. In that order. And then if you'd been out on the town, or if you'd finished with your boyfriend, or you were revising for exams, you'd have some supper. This might be some chocolate biscuits with a mug of cocoa. Or if you'd been out on the piss then it might be some curry or chips – or both.

The arrival of a hybrid meal called 'brunch' was the beginning of this unholy muddle. Some southern smart-arse went to LA or New Orleans and brought the idea back along with the hash browns and hominy grits and the waffles and maple syrup. It was the Eighties and suddenly Sunday dinner was officially off-message. Forget the roast beef and Yorkshire pudding, the new yuppies, Thatcher's children, went for bucks fizz, smoked salmon and eggs

Benedict. This silly brunch idea seems to have died out now, thank goodness. Or has it been reincarnated as the all-day breakfast?

Either way, the damage has been done. We no longer know what to say for the best. 'Let's do dinner' doesn't sound as good as 'Let's do lunch', does it? And while I've heard of ladies who lunch I have never come across a lady who dines. I would never have the nerve to ask someone round to dinner, it would sound so ridiculously posh, but what if I invited them over for their tea? They'd arrive at four o'clock expecting cucumber sandwiches and cake and a nice cup of Earl Grey.

You'd think our teachers would appreciate the finer points of English usage but they're even more mixed up than the rest of us. Kids don't have school *lunches* in the middle of the day, they have school *dinners.* Schools don't employ *lunch* ladies, they have *dinner* ladies. On the other hand, what happens if the kids don't sign up for their school dinners? They take a packed *lunch* in a *lunch* box. I give up.

When I first lived and worked in London I really used to suffer if someone invited me out for the evening. My first anxiety was always when I was going to get any tea because I knew that my friends probably wouldn't get round to having a meal until well after nine o'clock, if at all. Since I didn't live somewhere handy, like Soho or Mayfair, there was never enough time to go home, get changed, grab a bite to eat and come out again. What do you do under these circumstances? I'll tell you what you do: you go to a wine bar and drink. Then you might have a meal … or then again you might not. I've lost count of the times I used to stagger home to Wimbledon starving and legless. Up north we do things in the right order:

We come home from work.
We get some food inside us to line our stomachs.
We go up town (or downtown as the Americans say).
We have a few bevvies.
We move on and have a few more bevvies.
We have a curry on the way home.
We stagger home *full up* and legless.

❝ *The important thing which the southerners have still not caught on to, which is absolutely crazy, is that after going out to a nightclub you want a curry. And we'd always go for a curry till three or four in the morning ... When you went in there they'd take the handle off the door ... Northern Indian restaurants take the handle off the inside and then they put the handle back in to let you out, so people don't do a runner. But we'd be there till four o'clock. I mean, you can't get a curry at four o'clock in the South. That's one good reason to live up north.* ***Wayne Hemingway***

You can't tell me they don't do that in The Ivy too.

Currying Flavour

Who would ever have believed that curry would become the nation's favourite food? When the first wave of Asian workers arrived to work in the textile mills of Lancashire and Yorkshire some of them saw their chance and became entrepreneurs instead of factory slaves. And so it was that Britain's first Indian restaurant opened in Bradford in the 1950s. You wouldn't have been able to get a chicken tikka masala or a tandoori or balti dish there then. We invented them later, in the early 1980s, in the North. Manchester now has the country's biggest concentration of curry houses again, though Birmingham is the balti capital of the world, with over 100 restaurants attracting 20,000 visitors a week. OK so I haven't counted them, but they are bloody good.

In the Midlands we have a huge amount of Indian restaurants, as they do in Bradford. The balti meal and the balti restaurant was invented in Birmingham. It wasn't an Indian dish, it was invented in the Midlands. And they brag about their Indian restaurants, their Chinese restaurants in London. Yes, they've got some good ones, but the best ones are in the North. Absolutely. And that's just the way it is. ***Noddy Holder***

Birmingham has the best balti restaurants in the country. Some of the best curries are in Birmingham. Leeds and Bradford are the same. And we're actually much more cosmopolitan up north now than we like people down south to believe. They like to think we just do pie and mash and mushy peas.
Alan Titchmarsh

Lancashire Hot Spot

So in the North we like fish and chips and mushy peas, pie and chips and mushy peas, pudding and chips and mushy peas and we like curry and chips (but without the mushy peas). The other thing we like is pickles and we like them as hot as possible – hot enough to take the skin off the back of your throat. It might be something to do with the wind-chill factor, although I know of no scientific study. And I have looked for one. How sad is that? We pickle everything up north: eggs, onions, cabbage, small children …

Your taste buds change as you go further north and you take more vinegar. There's obviously something in the atmosphere, I don't know, but almost by osmosis you start to crave more pickles the further north you go. You wouldn't dream of having something like meat and potato pie without a side portion of pickled red cabbage. Oh, pickled red cabbage, you can barely buy that in the South, you know. ***Jenny Eclair***

Sometimes I think we just spoil you.

CHAPTER EIGHT

Quality of Life

I guess what really matters, and this will be true whether you live in the North or in the South, is your quality of life. This is a totally personal thing, of course, and everyone is different, but maybe there are some places that will make you happier than others. 'Happiness' is a scary sort of commodity but in 2005 Hewlett Packard did a survey that measured comparative happiness by sending volunteers to all cities in the UK to smile at strangers and count how many people smiled back. Nice work if you can get it, I guess. And their conclusion was that the happiest place in the UK is Manchester. Edinburgh came second in this 'happiness' poll and Cardiff was third. It will not have escaped your notice that not one of these three cities is in the South. So where does that leave Croydon, or Brighton, or Oxford, or indeed London? Well, Brighton came second bottom and London bottom on smile count – doesn't surprise me in the least.

Most quality of life surveys invariably put places in the southeast at the bottom of the list. But will the people who live there accept this? No. They cling to the pathetic belief that their crowded little corner of the country is pure paradise while persisting in their perception of the North as hell on earth. They think we never ever see daylight up here, never mind the sun, because there's a factory chimney belching out black smoke on every corner and we're all coughing our lungs out in the foul air. What a load of old twaddle.

Quality of life is different for everyone, and for some people who live in London I imagine they must value spending their journey to and from work squashed up against a total stranger with a personal hygiene problem,

Move along, you guys, London Transport figures say we can get another 19 people in there.

or spending more time than is morally acceptable in their cars in traffic jams. But for me quality of life is about being able occasionally to walk to work, or being able to put a wash on before I leave the house in the morning because I don't have to spend 90 minutes getting to work, or being able to go for a swim in my lunch hour or do a properly countrified walk on a Sunday morning out of my back door, or meet friends of an evening and not have an hour's journey home. But what do I know?

London

Living in London is worth looking at in detail because, let's face it, the people who live there are particularly snooty when it comes to the North. Here are some randomly selected horrid facts about our wonderful capital city:

- The divorce rate is double the national average.
- They have more road accidents.
- The capital boasts a higher proportion of people living in low-income households.
- They are more likely to be witness or subject to a crime involving firearms.
- Air pollution levels are breaking European law – the air quality on Marylebone Road was so bad in 2005 that it broke European standards by May (the limit is 35 days).

On the other hand … it's always handy for the latest Titian exhibition.

London hasn't always had such a poor record. Or has it? It was Samuel Johnson who famously said that when a man was tired of London he was tired of life, but I wonder what he would think if he came back to his beloved city

now, more than 200 years later. Because I would say that everyone I come across in London looks jolly well tired of life. They look tired full stop.

My sympathies are with Shelley, who felt that 'Hell is a city much like London – a populous and smoky city.' I hadn't realized that the Oxford Street sales existed back then. And I totally agree with opium eater Thomas de Quincey, who declared that 'a duller spectacle this earth of ours has not to show than a rainy Sunday in London'. The steady flow of white-collar workers streaming into the City from the Home Counties to do a day's work still look as miserable to me as they did to T S Eliot in the 1920s.

> A crowd flowed over London Bridge, so many,
> I had not thought death had undone so many.
> THE WASTE LAND, 1922

I had thought that William Morris had his head screwed on, was someone with a grasp of taste and decency, but I have had to rethink this since I found this little description of London gathering dust in our local library.

> Forget six counties overhung with smoke,
> Forget the snorting steam and piston stroke,
> Forget the spreading for the hideous town;
> Think rather of the pack-horse on the down,
> And dream of London, small and white and clean,
> The clear Thames bordered by its gardens green.
> THE EARTHLY PARADISE, 1868

What was he thinking of, as they would say now in *Heat* magazine?

London looks like it drains the very life out of everyone who lives there to me, with the exception of people who can employ a live-in maid and a full-time chauffeur, of course, or perhaps someone with so much money that they can afford to live in Mayfair. I'd be tired if I had to spend the time they do getting to and from work, and I'd look fed up if just about everything I did, whether it's go to the supermarket, the cinema or out for a Sunday afternoon stroll, involved pushing past hundreds of people who are trying to do exactly the same thing at the same time. Because London is full to bursting, officially full up.

There are currently 7.5 million people living in Greater London (an area of 1579 square kilometres), which makes it the second biggest conurbation in Europe after Moscow. In terms of overcrowding, for once the well off seem to be the worst off, since at 13,609 people per square kilometre, Kensington and Chelsea is the most densely populated area in the whole country … or it was in 2002, when someone

Welcome to London. See the sights – if you can move, that is.

last counted. No wonder there's always a queue at the deli counter at Harrods. With a mere eight people per square kilometre, the Scottish Highlands is the emptiest place in the UK. They compensate for this, mind you, by playing host to an insect population of 3 billion midges per human being.

Perhaps when Samuel Johnson was eulogizing about the elegant eighteenth-century salon society that he found so stimulating, London was a truly exciting place intellectually, and in some ways it still is, but during the Enlightenment, while the good Doctor and his fellow philosophers were pontificating in their coffee houses, most people in the city were chucking raw sewage out of second-floor windows, and dealing with Hogarthian-type scenes on every corner – prostitutes, beggars, brawlers, highwaymen, that sort of thing. No change there then. You get a tiny, tiny minority who have enough money to live in a three-storey town house in Chelsea, with more disposable income than the whole of Prestatyn, while everyone else has to put up with a poky little flat the size of a single wardrobe. For most people, London offers a pretty wretched experience, and this may explain why they feel the need to pretend to everyone else that living there is somehow more sophisticated, more interesting than living in the provinces.

“ *I would hate to be poor in London. I would definitely go north 'cos you get looked after better. I just think you know that you could be happier in the North as an old person with not a huge amount of money. I just think you could have much more of a laugh.* ***Jenny Eclair***

The North is often portrayed as somewhere that is awash with sink estates, where people make a living by selling heroin or crack cocaine to one another on brown-fill sites, but in fact there is more urban poverty in Greater London than anywhere else in the country. The proportion of the population living in low-income households is surprisingly highest in London (27 per cent), compared to the northeast (26 per cent). London has the richest households too, which is a fancy way of saying that the gap between the rich and the poor is largest in London. In fact, inner London has the greatest disparity – 29 per cent of the people living there are in the richest fifth of the national population and 32 per cent are in the poorest fifth. I am invariably gobsmacked at how much money there seems to be sloshing around. But that's mainly the two square kilometres known as the West End. Here's where you see the rich people, with their posh cars, and the designer boutiques, restaurants, bars and nightclubs that cater for them. But it wouldn't suit me.

❝ *I think there's a lot of people who live in London who have a more insular attitude and knowledge because they think that everything they need is in London, you know, 'cos obviously you don't need the Peak District or the Lake District or Blackpool or North Wales ... you don't need any of these things if you live in London because you can go to The Ivy.* ***Mark Radcliffe***

London dominates the nation's economic, cultural and artistic heritage; it gobbles it all up so that there's nothing left for anyone else. It's like an older sibling who always has to get its way and never tidies up after itself. Londoners would argue that the capital compensates because the city generates so much money for the UK economy – £106 billion to be exact (in 2002), which is an astonishing 17% of GDP. Some people in the City certainly get salaries that make your eyes water. I usually have to put my glasses on to check they haven't put the decimal point in the wrong place. But just about everyone in London earns more than their equivalent in the North. The standard argument is that London is officially the most expensive place to live in the whole country … my heart bleeds for them. Why don't they move up north, then, and give themselves a break? No – forget I said that – we don't want to encourage too many Londoners to emigrate because they might start bossing us about.

❝ *I think the reason why Londoners don't come to the North very often is because they're not welcome. Stay where you are. I'd hate for people to realize that the North is a nice place to live ... it's not actually, it's a bit rubbish. It's all flat caps and all we ever eat is pies. We've not even got Channel 4 yet so don't come, stay where you are, in your streets paved with gold. You'll be happy there.* **Justin Moorhouse**

❝ *How could you, in all good faith, sell the South to someone? You know, you say to someone, 'OK, come and live in London.' Someone says, 'Why?' And you say, 'OK, because you will pay three times as much for your house, it will be half the size as the one you left in the North. You will spend an hour and a half each day trying to get to work. Your whole life will be spent making excuses to people. You will be missing vital meetings and you will be saying, "I got stuck in traffic." Your air is dirty, your car is dirty, your skin is dirty. People are rude all the time.' How would you sell London to anybody?* **Carole Malone**

Dirty, noisy, and full of litter, which is all officially true. Londoners have more noise offences and dog poo inflicted on them than anywhere else in the UK. It also has the highest levels of sulphur and nitrogen dioxide and the Tube has so little oxygen that people regularly get panic attacks down there. And did you know that London has so many rats that you are never less than 50 metres away from one … and that's just the people in the office.

And don't talk to me about west London, where, in addition to all the grime and crime, you also have to share your life with a hundred jumbo jets flying in and out of Heathrow every day. This hell on earth starts at 5 a.m. and, if you're not used to it, at first you think there is a police helicopter circling the house looking for a killer on the run. It's only after the noise has died down for about 20 seconds before building up again exactly as before that

you realize it's a 747 up there in the sky and this pattern is going to repeat itself until 10 p.m. or whatever time it is that they have to stop. So you have paid a small fortune for a terraced house in the outer suburbs and you can't even enjoy a glass of wine outside in what the estate agents have laughingly called a garden.

Some years ago I bought a house in Brentford, which was the only thing I could afford. It was a smashing little house, in a lovely street with a park at the end, and only a short stroll away from the Thames. The only drawback … yes, you've guessed it. I would open my front door and – I'm not kidding – some mornings the smell of the kerosene was so strong it could knock you out, and the planes were flying so low that you could read the in-flight magazines.

Property in London and the southeast is so obscenely expensive it is difficult to comprehend. In 2005 Savills were selling a mansion in Windlesham, Surrey for £70 million – yes, £70 million. It had five swimming pools and enough garage space for eight limousines. They called it a 'billionaire's statement house'. How vulgar is that? But even if you wanted somewhere more discreetly tasteful, in Chelsea, say, then what would you get for your hard-earned? You're looking at more than half a million for a two-bedroom flat and you'd probably get little change from £150,000 for a studio flat with less square footage than a public phone box.

Perhaps it's no wonder then that compared to the North, people in London are unspeakably unfriendly.

> " *The trouble is, you learn to carry yourself in the same way and you learn very quickly that if you go round in London smiling at people and saying hello you'll get locked up or arrested. So you don't do it. Which is sad, really.* ***Alan Titchmarsh***

It could be that part of their ill-tempered manner and general unhelpfulness is because most of the foreign tourists who gravitate to this country don't get much further than London and the Changing of the Guard, so they do have my sympathy. They have a lot to put up with. Of course when we do want to come to London to see a show or to do some shopping, people from the 'provinces' have to compete with the foreign tourists for the rooms that are cheap enough not to take out a new mortgage to pay for. London hotel rooms are unspeakably expensive. They think charging £99 for a single room is cheap. Which means that most of us end up in one of those hideous small hotels in Earl's Court or Queensway, the sort of hotel that has a lift the size of a washing machine, a fire door every two yards, and a payphone in reception. The rooms are so small you have to shuffle your way round the bed to get to the loo. The last one I stayed in was so cramped that the only place they could put the telly was on top of the wardrobe at the foot of the bed, so to watch it with any normal focal length at all you had to prop the bathroom door open and stand on the loo seat. Nice.

There are some people who say one of the big advantages of living in London is anonymity. This means being able to walk down the street dressed as a parrot and no one much giving you a second look. I suppose if you're an A-list celebrity or a serial killer or someone who likes dressing in PVC crotchless outfits to get your kicks, then this might be handy. But for the rest of us? In fact, it has a reverse effect: it means that when someone does start to bother you on the Tube and starts spitting into their handbag to make you look at them, or is walking round with a sandwich board with an absurd attention-seeking message on it, you could do with everyone being a bit shocked, a bit supportive and helping you to get away from them ... not pretending it's normal.

Why do people live in London? Fairly obviously because of the jobs and it is a sad fact that this is often the only way we can kickstart our careers. Still, the great and the good are of the ridiculous opinion that if you haven't made it in London, you're second-rate. How stupid is that?

“ *The idea of coming to London out of choice seems to me to be absolutely crazy. Now, some people have to come to London and I have to confess that when I had to come to London in 1964 I believed that there would be a certain excitement about*

it. I was 29 and I thought, you know, London ... I'll go to the theatre three times a week, I'll eat out five times a week, it will be full of life, it will be one long party and, of course, life in London isn't terribly different from life in any other big town, except it's more expensive, the transport is hideous and you're more lonely.
Roy Hattersley

But times are changing and people are leaving London in droves, especially the creative ones, and there are more and more companies relocating in the North and taking their staff with them. Sensible people. And once people leave London and buy a nice house up north, they are invariably reluctant to return. Although some do take this notion a bit far …

I did live in London for a time. What would it take to make me move back? I think probably if there was an earthquake and there was a crack along the line between Bristol and Watford ... and then the North sank into the sea. That would probably make me move back to London. Probably – not definitely, but probably. I might think first if I could build an ark. ***Noddy Holder***

But you won't be surprised to hear that some people are so in love with London, despite all its hideous aspects, that they would never consider moving away.

I don't think anything would get me out of London and into a northern town. And if it were my misfortune to be transplanted, because of work or something of that kind, I think that I'd demand a private aeroplane at will so that I could get back to the South. ***Brian Sewell***

Could we maybe club together to get him one?

Living on Love and Fresh Air

One of the insults that southerners invariably sling at the North is that it is dirty and polluted. It's an image that's hard to shake off, because even though the shipyards and the pits and the mills are no longer working, they've left an imprint, both physically and psychologically. But you've only got to read D H Lawrence or Arnold Bennett or the Brontës – these northern writers show us that between the great cities of the industrial revolution there was always a wild, rugged and beautiful landscape.

The North has one of the biggest and most important areas of outstanding natural beauty in the country: the North Pennines. It is so important that it's Britain's first area to be awarded the UNESCO-backed status of European Geopark in recognition of its earth heritage. It is one of the most remote and unspoilt places in England. It's also a Special Protection Area in Europe for birds.

Our cities are now so green – take Sheffield, which has more than 2 million trees and over 200 woodlands and parks. It's said to be England's greenest city, but then Birmingham also claims the same. Has someone counted the trees? One undisputed fact about Sheffield, though, is that it is the only city in the UK to have a national park within its boundary. The Peak District National Park gets 20 million visitors a year … nearly as many as Mount Fuji in Japan.

These days, far from being polluted, the Tyne is one of the best salmon fishing rivers in Europe, and Merseyside has 30 miles of coastline and 22 miles of natural sand dunes and coastal woodland, which is the largest in England.

The thing about the North is that even if you do live in a city you are never far away from full-on countryside.

Never mind Richmond Park or Holland Park or even Hampstead Heath. Do these silly, pocket-sized urban spaces offer you a huge sky and a distant horizon with not another human being in sight? Do they give you a rushing stream, some snowflakes, and a tranquil, empty landscape where you can hear yourself think and the birds sing? OK, so you might not be able to see the latest movie within the first two days of its release, but when it does come to your town you are not going to spend the entire evening trying to find a parking space within walking distance of the cinema, are you? And you'll probably be able to afford to eat out afterwards without blowing a day's wages.

If all you ever relied on for your picture of the North was the paintings of L S Lowry, then of course you'd think the place was a dark, sooty mess, but gosh, how it's changed. The air is now vastly cleaner than in London – you don't have to wash your curtains and your hair every day, and most of the time you can get away with washing the car just once a week. What's more, the light pollution is infinitely lower up north. You can go out into the back garden at night and see a real ink-black sky with real stars forming real patterns; and if you're drunk you can see a dozen shooting stars a minute before realizing that they're in fact planes or satellites zooming overhead.

Getting out and doing healthy, fresh-air-type things is so much easier in the North. Whether it's cycling, rambling, fly fishing, mountaineering, orienteering or surfing, it's all going to be much easier to reach if you don't live in the nasty, bottom right-hand corner of the country. And on top of all that, our chips are bigger, our beer is cheaper and wheel-clamping is still a novelty.

The Lakes, the Pembrokeshire Coastal Path, the Dales, Northumberland's moors and forests – they are all so much

Real, open country – the view from my northern back door.

more accessible if you live in the North. And did you know that the Lake District is the nation's favourite place to propose? It's where Bill Clinton chose to ask Hillary to marry him and where Heather Mills said yes to Paul McCartney. But then I'd have said yes to Paul McCartney even in Cricklewood.

New Northern Money

People down south are convinced that we're still black-leading our grates, dragging the tin bath in from the yard for our weekly scrub-down and tearing up newspapers to wipe our bums in the outdoor lavvies of our back-to-backs. These prejudices make them feel a bit better about living in such an expensive, overcrowded part of the country but the truth is, the North has never been so prosperous. But I like this stereotype. Let's keep up the pretence that there's no money and no prospects up here. Why should we be colonized?

> *I like the idea that people think the North has not got any money and it's terrible. Good. Keep it hidden.*
>
> ***Justin Moorhouse***

'Where there's muck there's brass,' as the saying goes, but these days the wealth in the North is not created by coal-mining, shipbuilding or heavy engineering. The new wealth comes from the service industries, like retailing, entertainment and leisure or tourism. The Northwest Development Agency proudly tells us that 70% of all Japanese computer games are made within 30 miles of Liverpool. How's that for an amazing statistic?

When Harvey Nicks moved into Leeds and Manchester in the 1990s Londoners nearly fell off their chairs, but this was only the logical outcome of a process of change that had been taking place for over a decade. Almost by stealth, money has been pouring into new developments, initiatives and regeneration in the North but it has taken a while for the rest of the country to catch on.

> *If Harvey Nichols does stand for anything, apart from the attraction to a certain sort of footballer's wife, the fact that they did open a place in Leeds does show that the money's up there, the consumerism is up there. I mean, in a sense, if we're*

worried about the North being underestimated and underrated, the fact that Harvey Nichols goes up there is a good sign. I can't say that it fills me with joy but it's a good sign. **Roy Hattersley**

Drab is another word that southerners use to describe the North, but these days drab just doesn't fit any more.

❝ *Glasgow has cleaned its act up hugely – beautiful buildings, great fashion. There's nothing I can get in London that I can't get in Glasgow.* **Carol Smillie**

In Newcastle they buy twice as much champagne per head as they do in London. And did you know that the people of Cheshire are the most generous in the country when it comes to raising money for charity? Well, you should see the price of property in the county – there's a lot of new money there, all right.

You only need to drive around Hale, Knutsford or Wilmslow to see for yourself that these places look more like Hampstead than Hampstead itself – or Beverly Hills without the palm trees and year-round sunshine. Never

The new north – aiming for a lifestyle to rival Michael Winner's? Champagne delivered with the milk in Alderley Edge.

mind about Kwik Save or Argos, it's all designer boutiques, poncy wine merchants and domestic help agencies round here. And the houses! Some of these properties have got the lot: the swimming pool, the tennis courts, gardens landscaped and decked to death, state-of-the-art security systems. Every gate is electronically operated and every car in the triple garage has got a personalized number plate. It's more 'footballers' wives' than *Footballers' Wives.*

Property prices rocketing up has to be a good thing for us in the North. Apart from anything else, our friends in the South are less likely to trade in their oh-so-average three-bedroom semi in Bromley for something bigger and nicer … because they won't be able to afford to. However, although Tatton in Cheshire has the highest income per capita in the UK, the truth is that London is holding on to the wealthiest people. The place at the very top of the property price league is currently a road called Earls Terrace in Kensington (average price of a home there is £3.4 million), and the most expensive neighbourhood is Virginia Water in Surrey (£4 million). In terms of property prices, most of the nation's wealth is clustered in small pockets of central London, where the average price of a property is more than £1 million. But don't be fooled … houses in the prosperous new north are not as cheap as they once were.

“ *You'll get people whose perception of the North is* Coronation Street *– flat caps and clogs and things – and they sell their house and think, 'Oh wonderful, we'll buy a cheap little house up north,' and they come to Wilmslow or Alderley Edge and they get the shock of their lives because the property there is as much as it is in London. The way of life there is very middle-class.* ***William Roache***

People in the South who haven't been up north for a very long time still think of the North as a little bit poorer, a little bit behind the times, a little bit dismal, where people are more likely to work at blue collar jobs, or more likely to be poor. In fact, the North has steadily overtaken the South in terms of pulling itself out of its all-pervasive poverty, so although in the South people still earn more, on the whole it costs much more to live there, and I simply have no idea how anyone can afford to live in London.

" *Londoners don't think we have disposable income. They think, their attitude is, the bulk of people are living on the breadline. Of course, there's a lot of people who haven't got money to spend but that's the same all over the country.* **Noddy Holder**

Wales is for some reason the area outside of London that has some of the lowest living standards in the country: between half a million and three quarters of a million people in Wales were calculated to be living in a low-income household in 2002–3. In the UK, where 7% of households are still without central heating, the highest proportion of these turn out to be in North Wales … which may account for the fact that the suicide rate in Conwy is surprisingly as high as the Borough of Camden in London.

Areas like North Wales are examples of rural poverty, whereas large cities like Manchester Liverpool, Glasgow, Birmingham, Newcastle and Leeds represent the dynamic, prosperous north. You can tell this just by looking at the new building going on everywhere. The city skylines have been dominated by building cranes for over a decade now and with exciting designers like Wayne Hemingway on board they are beginning to look like cities with personality … and have bright prospects for the future.

And Work is the New Four-Letter Word

The North is getting wealthier but the South still has the monopoly on jobs – and the long working hours that come with them. Southerners work the longest hours in the country. People in London and the southeast work an average 43.5 hours per week and Londoners do on average 8 hours of unpaid overtime a week.

Business and finance still cling to the South and most companies feel the need to maintain a head office in central London for the sake of prestige (it certainly costs them a lot in rents and business rates) and that means having the magic central London prefix for your telephone number. Can you imagine how hard it would be to run, for instance, a couture business in Huddersfield? There is still a great deal more status and credit attached to having a London address as an HQ. Still business revolves around the capital and the southeast, and three quarters of the biggest companies are based in the southeast – most of them squeezed into the City. It is still the case that unless you work in London or have worked in London people think you can't cut it, you can't hack it, you're not taken seriously. Which means that sadly there are many ex-pats from the North who have no choice but to live in the South. And once they get down south they often intermarry with the natives …

But then when you've lived down south a bit and you go back up north, everybody thinks, 'Oh, you've gone all posh from being down there.' So you suddenly find yourself torn. And I'm always desperate not to be the professional northerner, who comes down here and sulks and says, 'Oh, I'm only down here doing missionary work, I'll be going back up there soon, you know.'

I came down as a sort of education, I came down to go to Kew, and I met and married a girl down here and so life, rather like John Lennon said, is what happens to you when you're busy making other plans. I ended up staying down here. And I go back a lot. I have to go back for my fixes. But I do notice myself when I go back up north slipping more into northern speak. Again the vowels just flatten and I get broader. ***Alan Titchmarsh***

Fat is a Northern Issue

Living in the North is more pleasant, that much should now be obvious, but how do we compare healthwise? Unfortunately, we do eat too many pies, which means that we are fatter and have a lower life expectancy. But it's not quite as clear cut as that and so here are some weird but interesting health statistics (according to the Office of National Statistics, 2005) to tickle your fancy.

Glasgow has the worst life expectancy in the UK (69.1 years for men; 76.4 years for women). And it's not much better for women in Liverpool.

Manchester has the worst life expectancy in England for men (71.8 years).

Blackpool has the second-worst life expectancy in England for men (71.7 years).

East Dorset has the highest life expectancy in England for men (77.7 years).

Kensington and Chelsea has the highest life expectancy in England for women (84.8 years). It must be all those facials.

Leicester or *Nottingham* inhabitants are less likely to suffer from headaches, colds, constipation or wind than anyone else in the country.

Swansea has the lowest gym membership in the country (1 in 20 people).
London has the highest gym membership in the country (1 in 7 people).
London also has more non-smokers than anywhere else in the country.
Women in the northeast drink more than anywhere else in the country.

The only health risk that they go in for in the South, apparently, is that they tend to work longer hours than people in the North.

I can't understand why you would work five, six days a week as hard as you do and probably get paid a bit more than you did in the North, but your house costs you five times as much. It costs you seven times as much to travel on the train or the Tube or whatever, the buses never seem to get anywhere. Everybody is busy, your mates live on the other side of London and you never see them. I just don't understand. ***Justin Moorhouse***

A Sense of Community

Perhaps more than anything else, more than any statistic or league table or new government initiative, the people up north continue to knock me over with their warmth, hospitality and friendliness. There is a real sense of community in the North … it's not that it doesn't exist at all in the South, that would be ridiculous, but in the North and in the honorary north there are still villages and towns where everyone knows everyone else. The new *Lonely Planet Guide* cites the people in the North as the main attraction – 'They're uninhibited, exhibitionist, passionate, aggressive, sentimental, hospitable and friendly.'

Village life isn't for everyone – living in such a close community can be a bugbear sometimes – but places like Humshaugh in Northumberland, for instance, are thriving. You can go to a whist drive, a WI meeting, a Pilates class or throw yourself into some amateur theatre and be busy every night of the week. Curiously, this is where, in 2005, a woman in her fifties was had up for making casseroles for half the village with dope in – strictly for medicinal purposes, of course – but no wonder so many people signed up for the cookery course …

Not far away, in Hexham, where I live, there is a knitting club that meets once a week in the Dralon heaven of the local cinema. We sit and knit and gossip and the younger members (those under 50) can ask someone older and wiser to help with the difficult bits. And we have a good old chinwag at the same time – that's what I call a community.

There is officially less crime up north than in London, despite the endless kitchen-sink dramas set up here. Alarmingly, the northwest is catching up fast and in 2004 government statistics recorded only 1000 or so fewer burglaries than in the capital. Whereas in the extreme honorary north, say on St Agnes in the Isles of Scilly, there wasn't even enough crime to register any figures on the chart at all.

Of course, as ever, if you have plenty of money then life in London can be a ball: some top-notch seats at the opera and a night out at the Limelight Club or The Groucho Club. Super. But how many people down south can really be said to have the kind of lifestyle that our very own favourite toff Michael Winner has?

You have to have a driver because you can't park anywhere ... If you can spend some money on a driver, everyone should have a chauffeur really. I do recommend it to them because it saves an awful lot of trouble. ***Michael Winner***

In the end, despite my articulate argument to the contrary, some people are just wedded to the South, don't really get the North, and are quite content sitting for days on end in their flash cars in a traffic jam on the Westway. Given that Michael Winner has been such a thoroughly good sport, I think I should give him the last word.

There is no money, no inducement, no incentive that could get me to live in the North. First of all, the weather is bad enough in London, I don't want it to be any worse, thank you very much, I don't want to be away from everything. I mean, if someone said to me you could have £100 million if you will live in the North for a year, I would say, 'Stuff it, stuff it for sure, not a chance.' ***Michael Winner***

Well, OK, not quite the last word ... my one really constructive thought about the way forward is to do some drastic rearrangement of the geography. It could prove to be more expensive than simply sawing the country in half as I suggested in Chapter 1, but how about sawing the country in half and then towing the bottom bit to the top and gluing it on? It would be an unfamiliar, funny shape, granted, but that way the South could have the longer winters, the year-round drizzle and the midges in summer instead of us. It might be a bit chilly but they can wrap up, and in the meantime we northerners can enjoy some unseasonal sunshine and start growing exotic fruit and veg. Doesn't seem fair? No, that's right. See how they like it.

Acknowledgements

I would like to thank Stuart Prebble whose clever idea the TV series was in the first place – and who got on with other projects while I wrote this book. But then he lives in Richmond, so what choice did he have? I am indebted to the celebrities who took part in the programme and the book and who were good enough to trust that a project with a title as mischievous as this one was indeed going to champion their beloved North – namely Carol Smillie, Alan Titchmarsh, Jenny Eclair, Shobna Gulati, Stephen Tompkinson, Stuart Maconie, Mark Radcliffe, Carol Malone, Kate Robbins, Justin Moorhouse, Roy Hattersley, Austin Mitchell, Wayne Hemingway, Noddy Holder, Louis Emerick, William Roache and Tony Wilson. And a special thank you to our three southerners – Michael Winner, Brian Sewell and Simon Heffer – who, shall we say, played the game, and who were good enough to be outrageously pro-southern, to help us make our point and to produce what I hope is an entertaining read. Many people helped to make the programme and the book both accurate and amusing – thanks to Keith Barron who narrated so brilliantly, also to Pip Banyard, Steve Seddon, Emma Beckwith, Fahima Chowdhury, Beth Matthews, Ann Hummell, Anne Leuchars, Neil Robinson, Hilary Oxlade, the Cumbria Tourist Board, the Liverpool Tourist

Board, and the many people who helped us pull a lot of things together to show off about the North. Thanks also to Maxine Watson at the BBC for commissioning the series.

Thanks to BBC Books for believing so passionately in the project, in particular Stuart Cooper and Sarah Reece who stuck with it, and Linda Blakemore, who designed the book and wrote the fab picture captions. This book is dedicated to Miriam Hyman, who researched the wonderful pictures. Miriam died tragically in the London bombings of July 2005, as the book was going to press.

Most of all I am indebted to the people in the North, whose warmth and kindness make living here so special, and whose cheery camaraderie help when the weather's filthy and you're so cold in bed you keep your duffle coat on. Thanks to my late father Gordon Holder whose favourite saying as a Brummie was 'Let the North do the worrying', which I always laughed at but never really understood; to my Brummie nearests and dearests – the Skoubys, the Thorpes, the Wrights and the Stevens; my friends in the extreme North, of which there are many; and to my beloved family in Hexham, Northumberland.

Picture Credits

BBC Worldwide would like to thank the following for providing photographs and for permission to reproduce copyright material. While every effort has been made to trace and acknowledge copyright holders, we would like to apologize should there have been any errors or omissions.

Air Images Ltd: 124. Alamy 17; 47 above; 62; 126; 133; 157; 171; 196; 200. BBC: 65; 90. Corbis: 38 above; 75; 91; 92; 103; 204. Empics (Martin Rickett/PA): 160. Mary Evans Picture Library/Town and Country Planning: 15 top. Getty Images: 15 centre and below; 37; 39; 47 below; 50 above; 73; 76; 83; 112; 120; 139; 173; 177; 180; 198. Judith Holder: 210. ITV: 50 below; 88; 151. Liberty Bell Productions: 9; 16; 18; 25; 27; 30; 35 both; 38 below; 48; 57 all; 66; 69; 81 below; 85; 108; 129; 130; 135; 136; 152; 165; 167; 194; 212. Margaret Miles: 81 above. Mike Parker: 20. Mirrorpix: 49. Rex Features: 94. Anthony Scot: 22; 183.

TON ❤ CLEETHORPES ❤ BIRMINGHAM ❤ STO
NEWCASTLE ❤ HUDDERSFIELD ❤ WALSALL ❤
JGH ❤ BARNSLEY ❤ STAFFORD ❤ MANCHEST
ERURIE ❤ HAWICK ❤ WOLVERHAMPTON ❤ ED
TROON ❤ SHEFFIELD ❤ HULL ❤ LEEDS ❤ HA
AND ❤ HARTLEPOOL ❤ STOCKTON-ON-TEES ❤
NCASTER ❤ AYR ❤ ELLESMERE PORT ❤ TELFO
ARNOCK ❤ BUXTON ❤ RUGBY ❤ TEMPAR ❤
ALASHIELS ❤ DUNDEE ❤ PAISLEY ❤ KESWICK
IDERMERE ❤ SCARBOROUGH ❤ BISHOP AUC
ARRINGTON ❤ CREWE ❤ SKEGNESS ❤ SPALD
TOXETER ❤ MANSFIELD ❤ WORKSOP ❤ MORE
K ❤ WETHERBY ❤ WIDNES ❤ CHESTERFIELD
NVERGARRY ❤ GREENOCK ❤ PITLOCHRY ❤ C
ELD ❤ SKELMERSDALE ❤ OSWESTRY ❤ LEOM
UFFTOWN ❤ SHIFNAL ❤ BRIDGNORTH ❤ WIC
GNA ❤ AMBLE ❤ PEEBLES ❤ STONE ❤ HEMS
HBY-DE-LA-ZOUCH ❤ HEANOR ❤ BARROW UP
ALVECHURCH ❤ WHITTLESEY ❤ PINCHBECK ❤
SLEY ENSOR ❤ CORBY ❤ LONG SUTTON ❤ CR
BEVERLEY ❤ SHERBURN IN ELMET ❤ OSWALD
CEY BANK ❤ ECKINGTON ❤ COTTINGHAM ❤
UISBOROUGH ❤ SHILDON ❤ CROOK ❤ HURV
PTON ❤ HEXHAM ❤ LOFTUS ❤ MARYPORT ❤
ETTLE ❤ SPENNYMOOR ❤ PREESALL ❤ WIGTO
ONNYRIGG ❤ NEWMILNS ❤ HALTWHISTLE ❤
A ❤ PONTELAND ❤ ROWLAND'S GILL ❤ MOR